15 *days*

of prayer with

DOROTHY DAY

15 days
of prayer/series

On a journey, it's good to have a guide. Even great saints took spiritual directors or confessors with them on their itineraries toward sanctity. Now you can be guided by the most influential spiritual figures of all time. The 15 Days of Prayer series introduces their deepest and most personal thoughts.

This popular series is perfect if you are looking for a gift, or if you want to be introduced to a particular guide and his or her spirituality. Each volume contains:

- ☙ A brief biography of the saint or spiritual leader
- ☙ A guide to creating a format for prayer or retreat
- ☙ Fifteen meditation sessions with focus points and reflection guides

15 days

of prayer with

DOROTHY DAY

Michael Boover

NEW CITY PRESS
of the Focolare
Hyde Park, NY

Published in the United States by New City Press
202 Comforter Blvd., Hyde Park, NY 12538
www.newcitypress.com
©2013 Michael Boover

Excerpts from pp. 45, 133, 166, 252, 285-6 from *The Long Loneliness* by
Dorothy Day. Illustrated by Fritz Eichenburg. Copyright © 1952 by
Harper & Row, Publishers, Inc. Copyright renewed © 1980 by Tamar
Teresa Hennessy. Introduction copyright © 1997 by Robert Coles.
Reprinted by permission of Harper Collins Publishers

Excerpts from pp. 163, 210 from *Loaves And Fishes* by Dorothy Day.
Copyright © 1963 by Dorothy Day. Reprinted by permission of Harper
Collins Publishers

Excerpt from *Therese* by Dorothy Day. Copyright © 1979 by Dorothy Day.
Reprinted by permission of Templegate Publishers, LLC

Uncopyrighted excerpts from the Internet site www.catholicworker.org.

Photos courtesy of the Department of Special Collections and University
Archives, Marquette University Libraries.

Cover design by Durva Correia.

A catalog record is available from the Library of Congress.

ISBN 978-1-56548-491-7

Printed in the United States of America

Contents

For David and Joanne O'Brien

How to Use
This Book

An old Chinese proverb, or at least what I am able to recall of what is supposed to be an old Chinese proverb, goes something like this: "Even a journey of a thousand miles begins with a single step." When you think about it, the truth of the proverb is obvious. It is impossible to begin any project, let alone a journey, without taking the first step. I think it might also be true, although I cannot recall if another Chinese proverb says it, "that the first step is often the hardest." Or, as someone else once observed, "the distance between a thought and the corresponding action needed to implement the idea takes the most energy." I don't know who shared that perception with me but I am certain it was not an old Chinese master!

With this ancient proverbial wisdom, and the not-so-ancient wisdom of an unknown contemporary sage still fresh, we move from proverbs to presumptions. How do these relate to the task before us?

I am presuming that if you are reading this introduction it is because you are contemplating a journey. My presumption is that you are preparing for a spiritual journey and that you have taken at least some of the first steps necessary to prepare for this journey. I also presume, and please excuse me if I am making too many presumptions, that in your preparation for the spiritual journey you have determined that you need a guide. From deep within the recesses of your deepest self, there was something that called you to consider Dorothy Day as a potential companion. If my presumptions are correct, may I congratulate you on this decision? I think you have made a wise choice, a choice that can be confirmed by yet another source of wisdom, the wisdom that comes from practical experience.

Even an informal poll of experienced travelers will reveal a common opinion; it is very difficult to travel alone. Some might observe that it is even foolish. Still others may be even stronger in their opinion and go so far as to insist that it is necessary to have a guide, especially when you are traveling into uncharted waters and into territory that you have not yet experienced. I am of the personal opinion that a traveling companion is welcome under all circumstances. The thought of traveling alone, to some exciting destination without someone to share the journey with does not capture my imagination or channel my enthusiasm. However, with that being noted, what is simply a matter of preference on the normal journey becomes a matter of necessity when a person embarks on a spiritual journey.

The spiritual journey, which can be the most challenging of all journeys, is experienced best with a guide, a companion, or at the very least, a friend in whom you have placed your trust. This observation is not a preference or an opinion but rather an established spiritual necessity. All of the great saints with whom I am familiar had a spiritual director or a confessor who journeyed with them. Admittedly, at times the saints might well have traveled far beyond the experience of their guide and companion but more often than not they would return to their director and reflect on their experience. Understood in this sense, the director and companion provided a valuable contribution and necessary resource. When I was learning how to pray (a necessity for anyone who desires to be a full-time and public "religious person"), the community of men that I belonged to gave

me a great gift. Between my second and third
year in college, I was given a one-year sab-
batical, with all expenses paid and all of my
personal needs met. This period of time was
called novitiate. I was officially designated as a
novice, a beginner in the spiritual journey, and
I was assigned a "master," a person who was
willing to lead me. In addition to the master,
I was provided with every imaginable book
and any other resource that I could possibly
need. Even with all that I was provided, I did
not learn how to pray because of the books
and the unlimited resources, rather it was the
master, the companion who was the key to
the experience.

One day, after about three months of reading, of quiet and solitude, and of practicing all
of the methods and descriptions of prayer that
were available to me, the master called. "Put
away the books, forget the method, and just listen." We went into a room, became quiet, and
tried to recall the presence of God, and then,
the master simply prayed out loud and permit-
ted me to listen to his prayer. As he prayed, he
revealed his hopes, his dreams, his struggles,
his successes, and most of all, his relationship
with God. I discovered as I listened that his
prayer was deeply intimate but most of all it
was self-revealing. As I learned about him, I
was led through his life experience to the place

where God dwells. At that moment I was able to understand a little bit about what I was supposed to do if I really wanted to pray.

The dynamic of what happened when the master called, invited me to listen, and then revealed his innermost self to me as he communicated with God in prayer, was important. It wasn't so much that the master was trying to reveal to me what needed to be said; he was not inviting me to pray with the same words that he used, but rather that he was trying to bring me to that place within myself where prayer becomes possible. That place, a place of intimacy and of self-awareness, was a necessary stop on the journey and it was a place that I needed to be led to. I could not have easily discovered it on my own.

The purpose of the volume that you hold in your hand is to lead you, over a period of fifteen days or, maybe more realistically, fifteen prayer periods, to a place where prayer is possible. If you already have a regular experience and practice of prayer, perhaps this volume can help lead you to a deeper place, a more intimate relationship with the Lord.

It is important to note that the purpose of this book is not to lead you to a better relationship with Dorothy Day, your spiritual companion. Although your companion will invite you to share some of his deepest and most intimate thoughts, your companion is doing so only to bring you to that place where God dwells. After all, the true measurement of all companions for the journey is that they bring you to the place where you need to be, and then they step back, out of the picture. A guide who brings you to the desired destination and then sticks around is a very unwelcome guest!

Many times I have found myself attracted to a particular idea or method for accomplishing a task, only to discover that what seemed to be inviting and helpful possessed too many details. All of my energy went to the mastery of the details and I soon lost my enthusiasm. In each instance, the book that seemed so promising ended up on my bookshelf, gathering dust. I can assure you, it is not our intention that this book end up in your bookcase, filled with promise, but unable to deliver.

There are three simple rules that need to be followed in order to use this book with a measure of satisfaction.

Place: It is important that you choose a place for reading that provides the necessary atmosphere for reflection and that does not allow for too many distractions. Whatever place you choose needs to be comfortable, have the necessary lighting, and, finally, have a sense of "welcoming" about it. You need to be able to look forward to the experience of the journey. Don't travel steerage if you know you will be more comfortable in first class and if the choice is realistic for you. On the other hand, if first class is a distraction and you feel more comfortable and more yourself in steerage, then it is in steerage that you belong.

My favorite place is an overstuffed and comfortable chair in my bedroom. There is a light over my shoulder, and the chair reclines if I feel a need to recline. Once in a while, I get lucky and the sun comes through my window and bathes the entire room in light. I have other options and other places that are available to me but this is the place that I prefer.

Time: Choose a time during the day when you are most alert and when you are most receptive to reflection, meditation, and prayer. The time that you choose is an essential component. If you are a morning person, for example, you should choose a time that is in the morning. If you are more alert in the afternoon, choose an afternoon time slot; and if evening is your preference, then by all means choose the evening. Try to avoid "peak" periods in your daily routine when you know that you might be disturbed. The time that you choose needs to be your time and needs to work for you.

It is also important that you choose how much time you will spend with your companion each day. For some it will be possible to set aside enough time in order to read and reflect on all the material that is offered for a given day. For others, it might not be possible to devote one time to the suggested material for the day, so the prayer period may need to be extended for two, three, or even more sessions. It is not important how long it takes you; it is only important that it works for you and that you remain committed to that which is possible.

For myself I have found that fifteen minutes in the early morning, while I am still in my robe and pajamas and before my morning coffee, and even before I prepare myself for the day, is the best time. No one expects to see me or to interact with me because I have not yet "announced" the fact that I am awake or even on the move. However, once someone hears me in the bathroom, then my window of opportunity is gone. It is therefore important to me that I use the time that I have identified when it is available to me.

Freedom: It may seem strange to suggest that freedom is the third necessary ingredient, but I have discovered that it is most important. By freedom I understand a certain "stance toward life," a "permission to be myself and to be gentle and understanding of who I am." I am constantly amazed at how the human person so easily sets himself or herself up for disappointment and perceived failure. We so easily make judgments about ourselves and our actions and our choices, and very often those judgments are negative, and not at all helpful.

For instance, what does it really matter if I have chosen a place and a time, and I have missed both the place and the time for three days in a row? What does it matter if I have chosen, in that twilight time before I am completely awake and still a little sleepy, to roll over and to sleep for fifteen minutes more? Does it mean that I am not serious about the journey, that I really don't want to pray, that I am just fooling myself when I say that my prayer time is important to me? Perhaps, but I prefer to believe that it simply means that I am tired and I just wanted a little more sleep. It doesn't mean anything more than that. However, if I make it mean more than that, then I can become discouraged, frustrated, and put myself into a state where I might more easily give up. "What's the use? I might as well forget all about it."

The same sense of freedom applies to the reading and the praying of this text. If I do not find the introduction to each day helpful, I don't need to read it. If I find the questions for reflection at the end of the appointed day repetitive, then I should choose to close the

book and go my own way. Even if I discover
that the reflection offered for the day is not the
one that I prefer and that the one for the next
day seems more inviting, then by all means, go
on to the one for the next day.

That's it! If you apply these simple rules to
your journey you should receive the maximum
benefit and you will soon find yourself at your
destination. But be prepared to be surprised.
If you have never been on a spiritual journey
you should know that the "travel brochures"
and the other descriptions that you might have
heard are nothing compared to the real thing.
There is so much more than you can imagine.

A final prayer of blessing suggests itself:

Lord, catch me off guard today. Surprise me
with some moment of
    beauty or pain
So that at least for the moment
I may be startled into seeing that you
  are here in all your splendor,
Always and everywhere,
Barely hidden,
Beneath,
Beyond,
Within this life I breathe.

Frederick Buechner

Rev. Thomas M. Santa, CSsR
Liguori, Missouri

A Brief Biography

*O*n November 8, 1897, shortly after the death of Saint Thérèse of Lisieux and six years after the publication of Pope Leo XIII's ground-breaking encyclical, *Rerum Novarum* ("On the Condition of Workers"), Dorothy Day was born in Brooklyn, New York. Little did anyone know that she would propagate her own "little way" in America, exercising a spiritual influence much like Thérèse's in Europe. Few would suspect she would take up the cause of workers and the poor, as Pope Leo had so hoped the entire Church would in response to the social ravages that accompanied rapid industrialization. Yet Dorothy would become a premier exponent of Catholic social teaching in America, and in many ways exemplifies the tradition in North America. She did not arrive

at or assume this calling quickly. Her discernment went through a process of development.
Her life story is quite striking in this regard;
telling her story is a good starting point for
examining her call to prayer, a call in which
we all share. At the turn of the twentieth century Brooklyn was a lot different than it is at
the turn of the twenty-first. There were vacant
lands, like the marsh where the Day children
played. The family did not lack love, but the
parents and children kept a cool emotional distance from one another. Nevertheless, Dorothy
felt close to her mother and was happy playing
with her precocious siblings.

Although the Days were not particularly
religious, Dorothy was. Her spiritual inklings
stood out from an early age. Their ties to organized religion were tenuous at best, attending
services now and again in different Protestant
churches. Yet these disparate and episodic
encounters with Christian faith made a deep
impression on young Dorothy. Within her was
growing a sense of a biblical truth to be had
and a sacred realm to be accessed.

Dorothy's father, John Day, a sports writer,
was subject to the economic fluctuations and
vicissitudes of the profession. His search for
steady employment led to a major move when
a California newspaper offered him a position
as a racetrack reporter. The Days left Brooklyn

for Oakland, where Dorothy passed a fairly happy period of her childhood, although she witnessed the physical destruction and human tragedy of the great San Francisco earthquake of 1906. The event was pivotal for Dorothy's formation as an agent of compassion. The quake uprooted the Days once again. This time, the family moved to Chicago where Dorothy spent her days reading voraciously and taking her baby brother John on long walks through the poorer quarters of the city. Initially, her family's new-found poverty embarrassed Dorothy. Fearing ridicule, she pretended to live elsewhere and entered their apartment building through a back entrance. Yet she also bore a ready solidarity with the poor and the immigrants through whose neighborhoods she pushed little John in his stroller.

The lives of ordinary people intrigued Dorothy. The poor, she discovered—despite what seemed overwhelming odds—made life bearable for themselves and others in the midst of squalor. The young observer concluded that despite their economic status, all people had inherent dignity. She saw an amazing resilience and creativity in the lives of many of her poor neighbors. Her discoveries on these walks roused in her a ready defense of the dignity of all.

Mr. Day soon found a good reporting job in Chicago. Having recovered financially the family moved to comfortable quarters in the more affluent north side, where Dorothy's father kept a fine home library that gave her access to many of the classics. She avidly read Dostoevsky, Tolstoy and Chekov. She read Hugo, Stevenson and Dickens, as well as American writers like Poe and Cooper. She was moved by reform-minded authors like Jack London, a determined friend of labor, and Upton Sinclair whose *The Jungle* brought to light the unsanitary and inhumane working conditions in the Chicago stockyards, spurring much needed regulation and sanitation in the meat-processing industry. Such reading taught her how writers could contribute to enlightened social change and aroused in her a culturally rich and morally critical stance toward those who would neglect the plight of the needy. Like the authors she read, Dorothy herself decried the condition of the poor and the state's lack of concern for them.

At age 16, Dorothy won a scholarship to the University of Illinois in Urbana, where she supported herself doing domestic work and baby-sitting. She befriended dedicated leftists whose revolutionary zeal for a new world impressed her, and joined the campus Socialist Party. After two years, Dorothy found studies not to her liking nor worthy of the attention they demanded, so she dropped out. With her family she returned to New York City, where she continued exploring her budding socialist leanings and calling as a radical writer.

In New York, despite her father's strong opinion that journalism was no place for a woman, Dorothy found work as a writer and took an apartment in Greenwich Village. Despite his obvious scorn for her decision, Dorothy sought to develop her gifts. As a discriminating reader she knew what it meant to write well, and the one type of writing by which she could convey her deep social consciousness was journalism. A socialist paper hired her, the first in a succession of leftist journals for which she wrote enthusiastically (*The Call*, *The Masses* and *The Liberator*). Dorothy fit in with the New York bohemian literary set, a band of writers in the vanguard of American radical politics.

Dorothy took up with the socialists', communists' and anarchists' artful yet openly propagandistic critique of American economic and foreign policy. Her friends and acquaintances included literary activists like Max Eastman, Mike Gold, Eugene O'Neill, Malcolm and Peggy Cowley, Floyd Dell, Jack Reed, Caroline Gordon, Allen Tate, Hart Crane, John Dos Passos and Kenneth Burke. Some were sympathetic to the Russian revolution, others to pacifism and anti-imperialism. Others were devoted to securing women's suffrage. All were committed to generating a cultural climate more supportive of change. Dorothy was smitten with the revolutionary fervor and bravery of individuals like Elizabeth Gurley Flynn and Eugene Victor Debs. It was an exciting time to be a young rebel.

Many of her friends—ardent unionists, suffragettes, struggling and successful writers, bohemians, and other cultural enthusiasts—gathered at bars; some drank heavily. Day herself could keep up with the best of them. Later in life, she was quick to downplay such "accomplishments" when they appeared in print. She was upset with Dan Wakefield, whose chronicle of life in New York City in the 1950s cited Malcolm Cowley's assertion that Dorothy had unflinching stamina with drink. She did not want to set a bad example. Paradoxically, perhaps, it was this garrulous and indulgent community that somehow helped her narrow the gap between professing radical faith and practicing radical deeds. Her friends had a discipline of commitment, an observable correspondence between word and deed. Before long, Dorothy was decrying the maltreatment of suffragists who were arrested after their protest at the White House in 1917. She too was jailed for the cause and joined her friends behind bars in a hunger strike. She learned the high cost of maintaining one's convictions—serious and sometimes cruel opposition. She learned that anyone who would challenge injustice needed two essentials: a sturdy disposition and daring.

The Palmer Raids of 1919 and 1920 rounded up many suspected leftist sympathizers among the newly immigrated; many were deported. Dorothy and her American-born literary comrades also fell under suspicion and their publications were investigated. By political intimidation, their political voices were muted or silenced. These experiences of suppression made a deep impression on Day. They served to both define and sharpen her growing critical consciousness and developed her growing sense of the depth of the social problems she and her radical peers were seeking to address. She also learned the challenge of changing oneself and taking personal responsibility. Securing even a modest measure of social justice demanded a great commitment.

Over time, Day's radical friends acknowledged her unspoken but increasingly evident spiritual sensibilities. Some suspected openly that Dorothy was too religious to be a good communist. While she shared her radical associates' disgust over an unjust and war-based economic system, she became increasingly skeptical that external revolution alone could address the deep-seated evils of inequality and violence in the American soul. Dorothy had been given a Bible in jail. During the hunger strike she took comfort in praying the psalms, which sparked her understanding that revolution had to begin within. Later in life, sure that anything less was inadequate, she called expressly for "a revolution of the heart." At the same time, she recognized the paucity of her own best spiritual efforts and took comfort that God would do for believers what they could not fully do for themselves. She likened herself and her spiritual kindred to the little boy who offered his few loaves and fishes to the Master so that the multitudes could be fed. If God would bless and multiply what this young lad had given, so too would God do for her and those who followed her way if they were generous enough to give all that they had, no matter how small it seemed.

Young Dorothy was complex. She was intellectually astute, worldly wise, and socially generous, but also had an intense need for recognition and affection. Her physical beauty coupled with profound unmet emotional and spiritual longings made her extraordinarily vulnerable to romantic involvements with the men in these social movements. She hungered for authentic intimacy, but these relationships

turned out to be frustratingly temporary.
Having discovered and appreciated the passion and joy of romance, Dorothy was doubly
wounded by the losses she suffered in her first
forays into affairs of the heart. Later in life she
described these episodes as moments of being
personally and morally adrift. She would have
had matters of the heart go quite differently
than they did.

These disappointing forays into romantic
love taught her difficult, painful lessons about
the lures and dangers of uncommitted love.
More and more, Dorothy recognized and
reeled from the excesses of a bohemian past,
including multiple failed attempts at relationships, including a much-regretted abortion.
She shifted her professional pursuits briefly to
nursing, was hastily married, and moved to
Europe where her short-lived marriage fizzled.
But there seemed to be other factors at work in
determining her direction—circumstance, or
resignation to her fate, or perhaps a sense that
God had chosen her for a particular communal
work. She understood that she had intellectual
gifts, but she also realized that she needed
direction, particularly in her spiritual life.

In the mid-1920s Dorothy fell deeply in love
with a biologist, Forster Batterham, and longed
for their union to be truly blessed. She hoped
this relationship, unlike her other romantic

involvements, would last. Dorothy feared she had been left barren following the abortion, but their common-law marriage proved fruitful with the arrival of their daughter, Tamar Teresa, in 1926. The unexpected conception and birth of Tamar brought Dorothy great relief and, even more, the joy of motherhood. She had high hopes. Yet Forster, an anarchist atheist, could not in principle (and would not in practice) accept the institution of marriage nor could he condone his lover's growing fascination with Catholicism. Although they did love each other, Dorothy's deep longing to marry Forster remained just a dream. Dorothy's desire to establish a nuclear family was not to be. Although they both welcomed Tamar and loved her deeply, politics and religion drove them away from each other. Dorothy always paid attention to families, and later in life was especially solicitous of Tamar's family and those of her grandchildren. Although she was never able to establish a family herself, she became the mother of many families. Once, referring to herself, she cited Psalm 113: "Who maketh a barren woman to dwell in a house, the joyful mother of children."(Ps 113:9 [DV]).

In retrospect, the purpose of Dorothy's early relations with radicals and her tumultuous romantic relationships became clearer. After her conversion to Catholicism and baptism in

1928, she exercised greater care concerning matters of politics and matters of the heart. She embraced the love of enemy over partisan love of friends and allies, and the love of the many over the love of one. Dorothy was sincere in her commitments to unconditional, unilateral love and community. Yet she expressed how dearly indeed it cost her, how these choices filled her with anguish. Her great gratitude for Tamar had propelled her toward faith. After her conversion, she looked at her passion and anger differently. As painful as it was to do so, she left Forster. All the injustice she witnessed in the world still incensed her, but she could hold that anger at bay, she admitted, more than she ever thought possible.

Mother and child set out on a new path together. Dorothy picked up paid work through script writing and later freelance work for Catholic publications. Her loneliness remained, but she found rest and stability knowing that she was guided by faith. Her recently published letters are filled with the emptiness she felt without Forster. She tried to escape the heartbreak by going to Hollywood and Mexico City, but the distance only made her feel more bereft, more saddened than her letters alone can convey. The partner she loved and who also loved her would not marry her and could not tolerate her attraction to faith.

What could she do? She became a tireless seeker after a better personal day for herself and a better day for society, a renewed social order. She would pursue such seeking, however, more on her own terms, an even more dramatic change than that of her conversion.

On the surface Day's conversion might seem improbable, but a closer look reveals the many accumulated experiences in her decision to become a Catholic. The unmistakable impetus, what finally pushed her over the edge of indecision, was the wondrous gift of creation she discovered in the birth of Tamar. She *needed* someone to thank, she said, someone to express her overflowing gratitude that New Life had issued from a womb she thought would never be fruitful. The "someone" whom she thanked, God, became an intimate who called her to thanksgiving and appreciation of the natural world, and this God called her beyond gratitude to a wonderful, most sacrificial vocation. Like Augustine did in his *Confessions,* in her autobiographical *The Long Loneliness* Dorothy traced her journey beyond personal discontent and spiritual malaise to a resting in God. She based her generous social vision in part on that personal spiritual experience. If she, a sinner, could discover new spiritual prospects, then everyone could. She based her choice to join the poor and marginalized on American city streets on her honest reckoning concerning the truth of our human condition. In one form or another, we are all poor. The blessed corollary to that truth, however, one that Dorothy came to know well and that lies at the heart of her vocation to change the world, is that every human person also shares in God's love. This "good news" can "make all things new." Dorothy learned that our very need elicits the love and grace of a loving Father who restores humanity and sets us free. That love and grace and freedom is the end or *telos* of the spiritual life.

At first, Dorothy kept her faith to herself. In fact, even as she began praying in churches frequented by immigrants, the very people who drew her to this Church of the poor, she had never met a Catholic face-to-face. Bit by bit, however, she sought out and formed personal relationships with the editors of Catholic publications who gave her the chance to support her child and herself as a Catholic writer, although one with an unusual pedigree.

In December of 1932, covering a hunger march for *Commonweal*, Dorothy prayed for help at the Basilica of the National Shrine of the Immaculate Conception in Washington, D.C. While reporting on the "March of the Unemployed" (organized by communists) that had descended on the capitol, Dorothy wondered and prayed about her own vocation. Specifically, she sought a remedy for her particular quandary: how to reconcile her faith with her passion for justice and love for workers and the poor. She prayed that she "might find something to do in the social order besides reporting conditions. I wanted to change them, not just report them, but I had lost faith in revolution, I wanted to love my enemy, whether capitalist or communist." [1]

At the same time that Dorothy was praying to find a way forward, a French émigré, Peter Maurin, a former Christian Brother, peasant and philosopher of labor, occupied himself with prayer and with work as a handyman at a boys' camp at Mount Tremper, in upstate New York. He, too, was hoping that he could discern a way to contribute to the common good. From time to time, he would come downstate to visit the New York City Public Library. The New Yorkers he met there gave his ideas for a truly Catholic way at best a mixed reception. One day, Dorothy had prayed to discover a holy work that would truly be her own; the next day, Maurin appeared at her apartment door. Dorothy's life and world would never be the same.

To understand Dorothy, a young convert and activist, we must also know and appreciate this new mentor of hers. Dorothy was decades younger than Peter, a pleasantly eccentric and brilliant Don Quixote-styled troubadour of the Lord. He was a master at appropriating the best insights of established thinkers. He also knew how to interpret and appreciate a wide range of critical thought from a Catholic intellectual perspective. He was a grand synthesizer! One New York City banker who Peter used to visit described him as "the most well-read man he had ever met." He shared with Dorothy his "long view" of history that helped her understand how to use her formidable literary gifts in shaping her own vocation in correspondence with a thoroughly Catholic worldview. Maurin showed Dorothy how to pursue a way of life based on the early Christian communal ideal. Their shared vision of the beloved community captured her attention and imagination. At first Dorothy spent a lot of time just listening, because talking was what Peter did most and perhaps best. Dorothy, moved by what Peter had taught her, became ready to act. In 1933, this mysteriously matched and holy pair founded the Catholic Worker Movement.

Maurin nurtured his and Dorothy's vocation and that of the many others who joined them in this nascent Catholic movement which was taking root in the suffering depths of the Depression. The movement offered rest and light in a weary and dark age, and flourishes still because of that blessed root and its ongoing mission to soothe the wounds of the least and to dispel the shadows of social sin with the light of the gospel.

Day spent a lifetime as a Catholic radical, serving with humility the droves of desperate poor who came to her door and crying out—as did the "Wobblies" (The International Workers of the World)—for "a new society in the shell of the old." She appropriated their motto, "An injury to one is an injury to all," to name the Catholic role in providing relief for the Mystical Body of Christ. In practice the "Wobblies" demonstrated a full conceptual grasp of Christian doctrine, with its rich Pauline imagery of the human body; if one member suffers, all suffer. What was true for the radical labor movements who promoted solidarity with the suffering masses was true for the Body of Christ. Dorothy's fully orthodox and fully radical claim as a Catholic to such solidarity held great implications for her and for the Church she had entered and was growing to love and serve. She would become a living example of Catholic social teaching taken seriously in an American context. She taught Americans what it meant to uphold human dignity and promote solidarity.

Peter proposed what he called "gentle personalism," a giving priority to the kindly relation of persons, acknowledging fully the sacred tie that binds us to each other. Maurin proposed his approach to social relation as the proper and much needed antidote to extreme self-interest on one hand and coercive collectivism on the other. He wished to avoid both a rugged individualism that neglects the common interest and a loss of the freedom and dignity of the individual. He saw the need for conscientious persons who would commit themselves with equal vigor to the personal and to the social. Individuals like this could forge a new vision that recognized with freedom and with love the value of others' needs. Peter helped Dorothy recognize this dual commitment to the individual and to society. It was a great gift that enabled her to continue working as a journalist, sure that by living out the social teachings of the Church she could at the same time decry injustice with her pen and *do* something about it directly.

The task that Peter and Dorothy set before themselves was no less than converting people from selfishness and hatred to personal and social responsibility, shaping a world where every person had the physical and spiritual means to live a dignified life. By her very life, Dorothy addressed the concerns of the universal Church. Her calling attention to the scandal of directing wealth to armaments instead of to worldwide human needs was deeply Christian, echoing Catholic social doctrine. For almost fifty years Day challenged her fellow Catholics, indeed the whole world, to turn from selfishness and pursue "the things that make for peace." She became a Catholic prophet.

After her death in 1980, The *New York Times* eulogized Dorothy as a "nonviolent social radical of luminous personality." She wrote seven books, over 350 articles, and under two different banners in The *Catholic Worker* over a thousand columns—"Day After Day" later became "On Pilgrimage." During his lifetime she published Peter's *Easy Essays* and after his death in 1949 continued to proclaim their shared vision. Dorothy had great esteem for Peter Maurin, who has been called a "second Francis" because of his devotion to Lady Poverty and the poor in imitation of the beloved *Poverello*.

Neither Peter nor Dorothy would be comfortable with the accolades they received after their deaths. Dorothy had no trouble acknowledging Peter's sanctity, but when someone suggested similar recognition for her she replied brusquely: "Don't call me a saint. Don't dismiss me that easily." These two "saints" never called attention to their own virtue. They did not seek holiness for themselves but for all. In dismissing her own sanctity, she intended a lesson for everyone. We are all in this together. None of us should dismiss ourselves that easily.

Ordinary believers can see in Peter and Dorothy an example of spiritual friendship. Their partnership exemplifies the life of prayer, poverty and work for sanctified social change that should be normative for us all. Dorothy's lay witness also testifies to a contemporary understanding of ministry. She fully exercised her gifts in the service of the gospel. She demonstrated that freely given and undaunted love is not only an idealistic way of life; it is pragmatic as well. Indeed, such love is the only remedy that really cures, the only thing that really works in the here and now even as we look to full union with Divinity in eternal life. Dorothy's perseverance in loving is a model of fidelity. When we struggle, we can surely look to her remarkable witness. To her dying day Dorothy embraced the way of Jesus, the way of the cross.

I had the privilege of attending Dorothy's wake at Maryhouse, the Catholic Worker house of hospitality for women on the lower East side of Manhattan, where she died. Dorothy's body was placed in a simple wood coffin made by Hasidic Jews in the neighborhood and set upon the altar in the chapel at Maryhouse, where a steady stream of mourners and admirers filed slowly by to pay their respects. Her visage was radiant, an unforgettable smile gracing her face, even in death youthful and unwrinkled. Her long loneliness was over. Even then, her physical beauty attested to the rest she had found in New Life. It was her last lesson to us — because we will be judged by how we have loved, we must therefore love in that measure. It is by love that all of us, despite our many failings and weaknesses, will find our way home.

Inspired by Dorothy's witness to Christian faith, peacemaker Daniel Berrigan, SJ, declared: "Dorothy Day, live a thousand years."[2] She lives and will continue to do so through us as we savor her influence and pray these fifteen days with her. As we enter into her story of conversion to a Christ-centered way of peace, we participate in the great drama of bringing about with Jesus the "new heavens and new earth."

Introduction

*T*his book offers readers a short profile of Dorothy Day and a guide to a season of reflection and transformation inspired by her words and her life. The text provides a framework for setting aside sufficient time for reading and reflection on Day's spiritual experience and connecting it with our own. By taking that holy admixture into our hearts and out into our social engagements, we can evaluate, undertake, and refine our labors of love in our own personal contexts. In fifteen days of attentiveness in prayer, we will meet Dorothy in all of her complexity and beauty and our own spiritual lives will be enriched.

What can Dorothy Day offer us? Each reader at prayer will surely find his or her own particular kinship with her. That said, there are broad outlines and dimensions to Dorothy Day's life that offer all fellow seekers and believers particular gifts, talents, and insights. She herself said so: "After all, the experiences that I have had are more or less universal. Suffering, sadness, repentance, love, we all have known these. They are easiest to bear when one remembers their universality, when we remember that we are all members or potential members of the Mystical Body of Christ."[3] The very heart of her life and work is this desire to reach out to all in a universal sympathy.

Dorothy claimed that whatever she may have achieved came about because she was not embarrassed to talk about God. This willingness to speak makes her a spiritual figure and guiding moral voice in confusing, even perilous, times. This radical American journalist turned Catholic convert at the onset of the Great Depression knew "by heart" the sad side of the human project. Familiarity with sin and the longing heart moved her toward grace and hard-got spiritual wisdom. Such wisdom can help us find our bearings as we consider our own sin and feelings of separation and alienation. We need not journey alone. We do better with friends and fellow pilgrims, especially spiritual trailblazers, by our side.

Day's signal gift is her path through stages of spiritual growth. These reflections will often refer to this. Dorothy's story exemplifies the value of slow and incremental spiritual progress. Spiritual awakening and intimacy with God grows through cycles and seasons. Seeing this dynamic of plodding, often painful growth and gradual transformation in another's life makes us understand and appreciate it in our own.

Christians are called to conversion (turning toward Love) and depth conversion (turning again and again and ever more deeply to Love). The themes in Dorothy's life and writing can help us attend to pursuing a holy life and working for renewal. The fecundity in her social apostolate depended upon the time Dorothy spent at the fonts of biblical truth and sacramental grace, and in prayer. She grew ever more clear-sighted and decisive. To build up genuine peace, she advised, abandon the works of war and like Jesus take up the works of justice and mercy. Dorothy exemplifies and teaches how, through prayer, we can find the strength to spend our lives softening our hearts so as to set aside not only our temptation to violence but any preparation for it. Dorothy calls us to full Christian pacifism.

Dorothy teaches that if we pray authentically we will seek peace by first being just and merciful ourselves. It will cost us to forgo vengeance and callousness and instead pour ourselves out in human generosity, in concert with Divine Love. We need each other's help in surrendering ourselves to the work of grace so as to bring about our own conversion. This book aims to provide just such help, a friend to a friend, a basket of bread for the long journey of personal and social transformation.

Dorothy's legacy is a sure sense of welcome to the banquet of love. We can sit and nourish ourselves with the humble and holy fare that Catholic Worker houses of hospitality have long set out at their tables. We can get food for thought at Catholic Worker "roundtable discussions" or sessions for "clarification of thought" whereby we refine our vision of the sanctified life. We get spiritual nourishment at the Eucharistic banquet table where the soul is fed her Savior by her Savior. Through manual labor we can express our own unique self-gift by furthering God's reign in a world that tempts us to a politics of scarcity. Dorothy does indeed set a grand feast for all who would sit at her table, a feast for the mind and the heart, for the body and the soul.

When I first learned of Dorothy and read her book *Loaves and Fishes*, I was most impressed by her love for all. Later, when I met her in person, I was moved by what I would call her "authenticity." She was deeply human, with an air of vulnerability. She actually had a shy disposition and spoke publicly only because she felt compelled to do so. It was not something she took to naturally. But once you heard her, you knew she was someone you could trust. Her doubts about the purported sufficiency of a social and economic order based on self-interest were well-founded and well-articulated. Even if sometimes communicated nervously, her faith in Jesus and her love for all were genuine and clear. She spoke with rare spiritual authority that included both simplicity and political *savoir faire*. She exhibited a rare combination of spiritual gifts.

It has been my privilege to be a student of Dorothy Day since October of 1972, when I joined her movement as a member of a fledgling storefront Catholic Worker community in Worcester, Massachusetts. We opened a full house of hospitality in 1974 and the work goes on. Dorothy's witness spoke to me and to my companions as we began our own "experiment in truth." Dorothy, so hungry herself for fulfillment, attracts the hungry. We too were as emotionally hungry as the physically hungry we served. My Catholic Worker colleague, Frank Kartheiser, stated: "We did not come to help the poor. We came to join them… for they were the only ones honest enough to wear their loneliness on their sleeves and we were that lonely too." Dorothy discovered the cure for her own loneliness in her fellowship of lonely friends, a fellowship that makes the friends less lonely. Dorothy spoke and still speaks to our lonely hearts. May you be spoken to and moved by Dorothy in ways that truly help you to grow in your own unique vocation. May you defy loneliness itself with the love and friendship offered by God and God's people.

In the pages that follow, Dorothy will guide you as you deepen your relation to God and to others. Through the key episodes in her life that led her to prayer, or in which prayer led her to take up initiatives at the Holy Spirit's behest, Dorothy can help you shape and integrate your own prayer and work. Thank you, fellow pilgrim, for setting your feet down on this path with Dorothy Day and me.

1

The Bible (and God) in the Attic

Focus Point

////////////

Our first sharing with Dorothy comes from a passage in her book, *From Union Square to Rome*, which she wrote to explain to her skeptical brother, John, "the faith that was now in her." She saw him as representative of a reading audience who wanted her to explain her unexpected conversion to the Catholic faith. She describes the profound spiritual discovery that came to her in the attic of her home during her childhood.

////////////

It began out in California where the family had moved from New York a year before. We were living in Oakland in a furnished house, waiting for our furniture to come around the Horn. It was Sunday afternoon in the attic. I remember the day was very chilly, though there were roses and violets and calla lilies blooming in the garden. My sister and I had been making dolls of the calla lilies, putting rosebuds for heads at the top of the long graceful blossom. Then we made perfume, crushing flowers into a bottle with a little water in it. Even now I can remember the peculiar, delicious, pungent smell.

And then I remember we were in the attic. I was sitting behind a table, pretending I was the teacher, reading aloud from a Bible that I had found. Slowly, as I read, a new personality impressed itself on me. I was being introduced to someone and I knew almost immediately that I was discovering God.

I know that I had just really discovered Him because it excited me tremendously. It was as though life were fuller, richer, more exciting in every way. Here was someone that I had never really known about before and yet felt to be One whom I would never forget, that I would never get away from. The game might grow stale; it might assume new meanings, new aspects, but life would never again be the same. I had made a great discovery.

From Union Square to Rome, 20

I had been reading books for a long time, since I was four, in fact. I can remember books I read, children's stories, and the fascinating Arabian Nights which I read when I was six. But this was the first Bible I had ever seen. It came with the furnished house, and I wanted even then to keep it always.

From Union Square to Rome, 21-22

///////////////////

*I*n discovering an old Bible in the attic of her new home in Oakland, Dorothy discovered a Friend whom she knew would accompany her for the rest of her life. Isn't it interesting that a little girl who was no doubt extraordinarily perceptive, but who through this seemingly chance meeting with a dusty old Bible one day, could make such a discovery? Even as a young child, it seemed Dorothy could intuit a call to shake off the dust to discover the lively and energetic Divine Presence beneath. This meeting of girl and Word in print and in person is important. Dorothy's childhood recollections resemble those in Thérèse of Lisieux's *The Story of a Soul*. Encounters with the sacred by these young women might inspire us to revisit our own childhood experiences to discover the hand of God at work in them.

Dorothy Day encountered many spiritual markers and clues until the moment in 1928 when she decided to become a Catholic. Throughout her childhood and young adulthood a variety of signposts intimated her call to a relationship with the Divine, but they did not lead her to a decision until much later in life. In retrospect, Dorothy could identify key experiences in her youth and young adulthood that lead her toward faith, such as discovering not only the Bible, but the God of the Bible. The words of the Bible itself drew her to the Word. Her enthusiasm about that discovery in the attic foreshadows her vocation. It certainly seems that this Word will work in this child and in due season produce good fruit.

In praying with Dorothy Day, we can sense the many passages or "Passovers" on the way to spiritual liberation and equilibrium. For Dorothy, the call to *metanoia* (change, conversion, transformation) arose in her youth. Examining her early "transitions" may help us appreciate the "rites of passage" in our own childhoods that have led and still lead us Christward. We can value our own particular vocations and our progress toward the reality and movement of God. God moves first to us, and invites us in response to make our own "pilgrim's progress." God can extend such an invitation to intimate friendship unexpectedly, as was done for the very young Dorothy Day.

Dorothy's journey to God unfolded over time. We should recognize and appreciate her childhood struggles and joys. Her trials as well as her moments of wonder and happiness suggest the venture of faith to follow. The seeds of the faith that Dorothy would come to embrace wholeheartedly were sown in her childhood. In that attic, Dorothy discovered more than a sacred book. She felt the presence of God. The One at the heart of it all called out to her, leading her beyond a mere object to the Subject that it contained.

Questions for Reflection

- ᘐ What childhood invitations has God made to you?

- ᘐ Can you recognize an emerging vocation in your childhood experiences?

- ᘐ What was your childhood experience of the Bible?

- ᘐ Does the Bible's power to mediate the presence of God excite you as much as it did for Dorothy?

ଔ Can you see that behind everything is
the One who is reaching out to us and
the One we have been waiting for?

ଔ What parts of your own spiritual autobiography have you overlooked?

2

A Shaking Earth and Intimations of Solid Heavens

Focus Point

In our second sharing with Dorothy, we search for the locus of our identity and security. For most who believe in Jesus, a time comes when our sense of security shifts from ourselves, others, and our environment to the person of Jesus Christ, to God. This may happen gradually. But it can also be prompted by a physical or spiritual crisis. Sometimes, such an earth-shaking lesson may occur through a childhood experience that upsets our familiar sources of security. The

51

experience of insecurity can be a grace that inti-
mates other ground to be found, other securities
to be gained. Insecurity can be disorienting, but
can also direct the insecure in another, better
direction. In *From Union Square to Rome*, Dorothy
describes what she learned from her experience
of the great San Francisco earthquake.

//////////////

What I remember most plainly
about the earthquake was the human
warmth and kindliness of everyone
afterward. For days refugees poured
out of burning San Francisco and
camped in Idora Park and the racetrack
in Oakland. People came in their night
clothes; there were new-born babies.

Mother had always complained
before about how clannish California
people were, how if you were from the
East they snubbed you and were loathe
to make friends. But after the earthquake everyone's heart was enlarged
by Christian charity. All the hard crust
of worldly reserve and prudence was
shed. Each person was a little child in
friendliness and warmth.

Mother and all our neighbors were
busy from morning to night cook-
ing hot meals. They gave away every
extra garment they possessed. They
stripped themselves to the bone in

·

giving, forgetful of the morrow. While the crisis lasted, people loved each other. They realized their own helplessness while nature "travaileth and groaneth." It was as though they were united in Christian solidarity. It makes one think of how people could, if they would, care for each other in time of stress, unjudgingly, with pity and with love.

From Union Square to Rome, 24

////////////////

*T*he April 1906 earthquake that struck San Francisco made a deep impression on Dorothy. She was eight years old, living happily with her family in pleasant surroundings in Oakland. During the earthquake itself, Dorothy found herself alone. Her family were attending to one another but somehow left Dorothy by herself in the shaking house, her bed sliding across the room. Amid tragedy she felt abandoned and alone. This solitary experience in grave circumstances made her question the nature and source of security. Perhaps this is the event that moved Dorothy to pray the prayer of the abandoned, the lost and the rejected. In later years she wrote about "poverty and precarity" (that is, the precarious nature of life itself) with an authority that comes from a felt sense of what a person can and cannot hold on to, with a first-hand experience that the constant threat of shaky ground is a part of human experience. Such a recognition can drive a child to interior resources--indeed to intuitions of God dwelling in the depths.

Crisis can provoke the search for a deeper source of security and can give birth to the discovery of what it means to truly love your neighbor. At the age of eight, Dorothy underwent a major spiritual transformation. The experience of abandonment traumatized her, but witnessing the outpouring of human kindness by the many who responded to fellow quake victims consoled and inspired her. The earthquake made Dorothy share in the displacement of wounded humanity but it also made her realize the deep human drive to pour out kindness, especially in difficult times. She noted how that time of shared suffering inspired people to rise to their higher selves and how the crisis itself elicited compassion and engagement, indeed allowing people to demonstrate the "better angels" of their nature.

In the May 1952 edition of *The Catholic Worker*, Dorothy addresses the predicament we face when we protect ourselves from the suffering of others. She suggests that if we wish to respond to life's realities and challenges we need to place ourselves in contact with suffering intentionally. She wrote:

We need always to be thinking and writing about poverty, for if we are not among its victims its reality fades from us. We must talk about poverty, because people insulated by their own comfort lose sight of it. And maybe no one can be told; maybe they will have to experience it. Or maybe it is a grace which they must pray for. We usually get what we pray for, and maybe we are afraid to pray for it. Yet I am convinced that it is the grace we most need in this age of crisis, this time when expenditures reach into the billions to defend "our American way of life." Maybe this defense itself will bring down upon us the poverty we are afraid to pray for.

When we have to let go of what surrounds us and consider what remains, the ground of our own anthropological identity can shift and leave us in a distinctly new place. This seems to have been part of what Dorothy experienced during the quake and its aftermath. As the young Dorothy stood with victims of that shaky ground in San Francisco she discovered another, spiritual ground upon which to set her pilgrim feet.

The promised land of the Bible cannot be seen by those about to set out for it. Still, we begin by following cues we cannot even see, then as new ways of seeing insinuate themselves we come to "see with the eyes of faith." While the eight-year-old Dorothy did not achieve a fullness of spiritual sight, she caught a glimpse of what was at stake regarding our fragile human condition, the transitory nature of things that we take for granted. Dorothy came to understand not only loss, but also of the presence and possibility for good. In the thick of a precarious life, a human and Christian choice is always possible. From the thicket of a battered, tattered humanity arising from the shambles of a trembling earth, she could glimpse and even grasp a seemingly strange path to security—the ethereal Eternal. Dorothy offers us the opportunity to catch and learn from that glimpse too.

Questions for Reflection

- ⚘ Which of your childhood experiences demonstrates how in and through crisis God has been leading you along paths of learning?

- ⚘ We have "no lasting city" in this life. Where do you find your new and heavenly Jerusalem, from which streams mutual concern and eternal life?

- ⚘ On what can you really depend?

- ⚘ How do the lessons that Dorothy learned from the quake apply to you?

- ⚘ Dorothy embraced voluntary poverty in order to reckon with the fragility of the human condition itself (we are always on shaky ground) as well as to embrace the One who offers true stability—Emmanuel, God with us. How can you embrace poverty in your own circumstances? How would doing so change your life?

3

The Noise and Impetuousness of Youth

Focus Point

Youth and young adulthood pose many wonders and challenges. Unruly energies within and around us tend to overwhelm, leading us to experiment and to dare. At the same time, we feel the need to channel or direct these energies. This time of life can be exciting and adventurous, but also confusing and daunting. Sometimes, after these great joys and great struggles have run their course, we reflect on our need for greater maturity, for clearer and better direction by which to negotiate full adulthood. In her own growth toward adulthood, Dorothy was no stranger to struggle. Pregnancy offered her a clear invitation to recognize that someone beyond the self was beckoning. What can we learn from Dorothy with child?

////////////

My child was born in March at the end of a harsh winter. In December I had to come in from the country and take a little apartment in town. It was good to be there, close to friends, close to a church where I could stop and pray. I read the Imitation of Christ a great deal. I knew that I was going to have my child baptized a Catholic, cost what it may. I knew that I was not going to have her floundering through many years as I had done, doubting and hesitating, undisciplined and amoral. I felt it was the greatest thing I could do for a child.

From Union Square to Rome, 131

////////////

*O*ur daughter, Alta, is an opera singer. Dorothy once said that if she were ever to be reincarnated, she'd like to come back as an opera singer! Occasionally, I have thought that Dorothy would really like our daughter, and

would have enjoyed her lifestyle immensely.
Some years ago Alta won a music scholarship
to Skidmore College in Saratoga Springs, New
York. At her graduation, as president of the
Honor Society, she gave her fellow graduates
a little talk. She began by thanking her mom
for putting up with her loud and undisciplined
voice until she found a way to channel what
I would call "the noise of her youth" into an
operatic frame. Her fellow students were nod-
ding in recognition. Many were feeling a bit
of trepidation regarding their pending work
lives and lives in general as they pondered
their immediate futures. She also told them, "I
would be remiss in my presidential duties if I
did not tell you: "Relax, it's going to be OK."
They applauded with delight at these surprisingly consoling words. Dorothy would have
appreciated Alta's message. Like Alta, she had
finally found the vehicle with which to channel
"the noise of her youth" — not opera singing,
as much as she would have liked to do that,
but the life of a believer and activist and writer.
Dorothy was grateful that God and others
bore with her youthful excesses and enthu-
siasms. Her own experience gives Dorothy a
useful perspective for consoling others whose
journeys have been more raucous than most.
In his *Confessions* Augustine could forgive and
console sinners because he recognized their

youthful sin and foibles. In the same way, Alta
and Dorothy articulate a journey of conversion
that is the product of a rare gift — the combination of experience and formational influences
that through grace manage to channel ren-
egade energies into a maturity for which all are
ultimately grateful.

The gift of discipline called both Dorothy
and Alta to funnel their scattered energies into
a unitary stream, making a vast difference in
the nature and quality of their lives, and those
around them. Jesus teaches his followers to be
"pure in heart." That requires a singularity of
vision. When our energies are scattered and
we hear a cacophony of mixed and distress-
ing voices (even within us), it takes a special
effort and openness to accept those graces that
enable us to focus our attention on the knowledge and love of Christ and to integrate in Him
the voices within and outside of ourselves.

Like Saint Augustine, in her youth Dorothy
Day was an intelligent yet troubled seeker. She
offers, as does Augustine, an authoritative
voice regarding the cry of the lonely pilgrim.
She describes perceptively the yearnings of
the hungry heart. Like Augustine, she cries
out to God from a place of spiritual and emotional desolation and writes eloquently about
it. She addressed the physical and spiritual
hungers of her readers. In the "messiness, the

untidiness" of life, Christ was her solace, the source of a Divine Life that could sustain any hungry heart. Upon arriving at a greater purity of heart, as did Augustine, Dorothy sang a song of gratitude. Her journey from radical Bohemianism and youthful hedonism was difficult. The boundary that marked off the change was her pregnancy. Thanksgiving rose up in her when she felt an invitation to a more disciplined life.

All journeys of self-effacement involve a kind of death and a belief that the victory of Love brings relief. As Dorothy journeyed to greater discipline, along with the child within her she also bore sympathy with the young in their struggles with passion and anger. But she also could be impatient when young people acted rashly, and sought to teach them the need for difficult but necessary labor for change: "Young people say, 'What is the sense of our small effort?' They cannot see that we must lay one brick at a time, take one step at a time." She wanted to address young people's impatience and blindness to spare them the sad lessons she had learned the hard way. In a letter to a young worker at the Rochester, New York house, she conveyed her sadness that the undisciplined young people of the sixties would have to learn the hard way, particularly regarding sexual matters. She wanted to help but also acknowledged that life lessons had to be learned first-hand. Sometimes responsibility can be realized only through suffering.

Dorothy strode away from the licentiousness that had marred her youth toward a self-discipline marked by a conversion to the Divine Will and Law of Love, aptly described in a well-known hymn: "Freedom can be found, laden down, under the weight of the wood." Discipline left Dorothy's soul free. At one point in her spiritual life she accepted an invitation to become a Benedictine lay oblate at Saint Procopius Abbey in Lisle, Illinois. This fellowship with vowed monks and fellow laity who adhered to a Rule—a way of living with Christian faith and integrity—further refined her vocation. Dorothy reached for the rich spiritual resources of the Church's lived traditions, as in the Rule of Saint Benedict. Her immersion in the wisdom traditions of Catholic saints and sages became evident as she cited these grand figures in her articles for *The Catholic Worker*. In every issue, their holy sayings punctuated the salty social pages of the paper with interior light. Dorothy drew upon the wisdom of the ages, and some young would follow her example. A good many today still do.

Questions for Reflection

- ☜ When have you felt the need to tame your unruly energies?

- ☜ When has a call to discipline reflected the workings of grace?

- ☜ How might you help others maintain hope that "God can conquer our shadows"?

- ☜ Who has been patient with you when you needed it?

- ☜ What saints or sages have influenced you so deeply that you often recall their words and example?

- ☜ What have you cherished from the past? What do you prize now?

- ☜ What rules of life might help you measure and refine the quality of your own discipleship?

4

An Ever-Expanding Horizon

Focus Point

Sometimes we reach a plateau, a moment when insights and graces make us appreciate our difficulties and expand our hearts. As we set our gaze on a wider horizon, our inner landscapes also expand. This new perspective sometimes comes through synthesizing our own varied experiences, sometimes through the shared insight of a significant other. In her mid-thirties, Dorothy was ready to take a higher, wider view of the political and spiritual landscape within and around her. When she prayed that she might achieve the vision of a greater love, God sent her a personal guide in the person of Peter Maurin. What can we learn from Dorothy's readiness to welcome a new vision, her willingness to entertain a wider horizon?

////////////

I pray because I am happy, not because I am unhappy. I did not turn to God in unhappiness, in grief, in despair—to get consolation, to get something from God. I was praying because I wanted to thank God. No matter how dull the day, how long the walk seemed, if I felt sluggish at the beginning of the walk, the words I had been saying insinuated themselves into my heart before I had finished, so that on the trip back I neither prayed nor thought, but was filled with exultation...My very experience as a radical, my whole make-up, led me to want to associate myself with others, with the masses, in loving and praising God.

The Long Loneliness, 133

////////////////

*D*ay's life-long "pilgrimage" to God can help us hear the call to take a longer view of our personal histories, to appreciate the "long-distance running" typical of authentic Christian spiritual journeys. Dorothy can help us recognize that conversion is ongoing and that the spiritual venture is open-ended. "Deep calls unto deep," the psalmist sings. A shared communion with the Christ of the ages leads us into the profoundest regions of our inner being. Peter Maurin was able to help Dorothy because he himself was well attuned to those depths. His own faith journey had taken him from his deep roots in the very soil and the folk culture of southern France to Paris, Canada, Chicago and eventually New York where the editor of *Commonweal* magazine suggested that he look Dorothy up, because they had much in common. By coincidence, on the feast of the Immaculate Conception, after covering a communist-led hunger march for the Catholic periodical *America*, Dorothy prayed to find a way to remain Catholic while maintaining her solidarity with and love for the poor and working people. She begged God to show her how she could alleviate the suffering of those she had come to recognize as the Body of Christ on earth. She understood that she could pray for them each day at Mass, but only in the light of Peter's vision did she realize that she could share the love of God for all with everyone.

Coming from southern France, Peter carried with him a profound sense of a sanctified and agricultural social order based on the sacramental life of the Church, an appreciation that he combined with the insight of

luminaries and visionaries who had diagnosed
the crisis of the West. That crisis consisted in a
drive for acquisition, systemic and systematic
selfishness, the neglect of cherished founda-
tions, of misbegotten and misplaced ideals,
of disoriented masses. Peter had met Christ,
whose person and Gospel brought a new day.
He had become convinced that Catholic scholars would have to be more involved in the apostolate in order to "blow the dynamite" of the
Christian evangel and thus make dynamic the
gospel message. Dorothy had the energy and
the intellectual acumen needed to take Peter's
notion of engaged Catholic scholarship into
the world. She was the answer to Peter's prayer
as much as he was to hers.

Dorothy sought to put into action the
new faith which she felt within, a new light
and bearing for which she felt grateful. As a
response, she wanted to bear the good news
to America's poor and working class as a
Catholic, but she did not know how to do it.
She found a way through Peter, a Catholic
who shared her critique of ruthless capitalism,
but with a twist. He was most gentle, deeply
person-oriented, and unflappably positive. All
these attributes led Dorothy to describe Peter
aptly — "as good as bread." She was convinced
that "our problems stem from our acceptance
of this filthy, rotten system," as did Peter, who

offered something beyond mere reaction. He
called for round table discussions, for houses
of hospitality, and for Catholic communes and
agronomic universities. His "long view" of
history provided the visionary lens through
which to perceive these new realities. His
view bespoke a reality "so old that it looks like
new," and it manifested itself as a movement of
immense appeal because it was neither just old
nor just new… it was a kind of a "new" old—as
old as the charity Christ dispensed to the suffering he met on the dusty roads of Palestine,
but recast in the American setting of the early
thirties. A visionary and an energetic convert
came together in their mutual openness, each
influencing the other through the workings
of the Holy Spirit! The world has not been the
same since.

Dorothy was drawn to the wonder of traditional Catholicism, to the mystical tradition
and later to those who spoke for that tradition
and with whom she identified—Catherine
of Siena, Teresa of Avila, Thérèse of Lisieux,
and Brother Lawrence. The Catholic Worker
creatively blended the traditional elements
with openness to the needs and vicissitudes
of a particular social era. This movement's
vista grew ever wider, its unique perspective
shaped through the interpretive lenses of the

saints. Dorothy and Peter's horizon can help us widen our own.

Questions for Reflection

- ✎ How would your life change if you took a "long view" of history and saw your life as a "pilgrimage"?

- ✎ Which forebears serve as your witnesses, teachers and guides, and influence your own journey of faith?

- ✎ How can your faith life become an ever-deepening collaboration with other members of the Mystical Body?

- ✎ How can you grow by expanding your horizons?

- ✎ How can you, as Dorothy did, draw closer to and find more comfort from the Catholic mystical tradition?

- ✎ Which guides might help you along "the way" in your journey of faith, hope and love?

5

The Power of Prayer

Focus Point

Through prayer we encounter a mysterious reality; we meet Ultimate Mystery. Interestingly, some who pray claim to have received or experienced immediate responses "clear as a bell" from the Voice on High. Others describe their experience of prayer as a kind of waiting, a painstaking process of keeping vigil. Here prayer is shrouded in mystery, a dwelling in the darkness of faith. One familiar metaphor for this state is being lost (and thereby found) in a "cloud of unknowing." Both experiences of prayer, however, have power—one more direct and conceptual, the other more subtle and allusive—to communicate

with God. In her spiritual life Dorothy experienced both types. What has prayer been for you?

///////////////

> There I offered up a special prayer, a
> prayer which came with tears and with
> anguish, that some way would open up
> for me to use what talents I possessed
> for my fellow workers, for the poor.

The Long Loneliness, 166

///////////////

*I*n December, 1932, after covering a hunger
march by the desperately poor and unemployed in Washington DC, Dorothy returned
to New York. While in Washington, she had
prayed earnestly at the National Shrine on the
feast of the Immaculate Conception. Upon
returning to her apartment, she found Peter
Maurin waiting for her. Meeting Maurin immediately upon her return made Dorothy realize
that the prayer she had raised the previous day
indeed had been most graciously heard. She
came to see Peter as her Heaven-sent guide. He
demonstrated for her a daring Catholic witness
in response to the social cruelties of the Great
Depression. Peter was the teacher Dorothy
needed; Dorothy was the student Peter needed.
Peter's life and wisdom expressed the qualities
she yearned to embrace.

Maurin came from Languedoc, in southern France, a deeply Catholic area. He blended peasantry with scholarship. He followed Christ's example by serving the poor, yet had a deeply contemplative and prayerfully contented nature. He felt deeply that the land was sacred, yet had a strong attraction to the urban poor. He found nobility in manual work, yet read voraciously. Peter knew intimately both the rhythms of rural life and the Catholic intellectual tradition of social thought that he learned and taught as a member of the Christian Brothers. His interest in social change arose through his involvement with reform and renewal movements such as *Le Sillon (The Furrow)* when he was a teacher in Paris.

Having grown up on a farm, Peter lived close to the Source (God) and sources (what God has given), yet agitated for the common good with urban activists and propagandists. Unlike his reform-minded contemporaries, however, Peter had a vision and maturity of thought marked by the ability to link perspectives seemingly opposed to one another, loyalty to the church even though it often disappointed him, interest in general and integrative education even though he recognized the appeal and possible usefulness of specialization, and an abiding sense that life was essentially Holy, a gift and sacred trust in a cultural milieu that often sidelined or blunted or minimized the sense of the sacred. Both scholar and worker himself, Maurin modeled the ideal of threading the intellectual's clarified thought with the worker's muscle, thereby giving ennobled thought the momentum to generate needed change, to making the ideal become real. Yet Peter proposed an even higher ideal. He called scholars to become workers and workers to be scholars. If thought and action could be wed in each person, a new and blessed community of scholar-workers would come to life. Peter envisioned houses of hospitality where the poor would be fed, clothed and sheltered at no cost. Communard farmers would build and refine a Catholic culture and economy on the land. This vision would be articulated in a newspaper that would offer ordinary workers a sanctified vision of a Catholic social order based on prayer, study, and agriculture as implied in biblical teaching and Church doctrine. Personal holiness and initiatives to serve the needy would usher in a new day. The movement Peter Maurin envisioned was characterized by faith, work, voluntary poverty, life on the land, a revival of craft labor and village life, along with a renewed sense of lay vocation. What Peter brought to Dorothy was the fruit of the heartfelt prayer she raised to God in the crypt of the national shrine's still unfinished basilica. Such prayer should teach us to be careful what we pray for. We just might get it!

Questions for Reflection

- ৫ঃ Have you prayed from the crypt of your own heart with a truly pleading faith?

- ৫ঃ How might God meet your needs for direction and hope?

- ৫ঃ When has the Spirit of God reached you through a teacher who has made his or her own profession of faith?

- ৫ঃ When have you discerned the finger of God in the events of your everyday life?

- ৫ঃ When has God worked in your life through an unexpected guest or visitor?

- ৫ঃ How might you make space in your life for prayer?

- ৫ঃ In which churches, chapels or other places of devotion do you feel that you can speak to God?

6

Poverty and Hope

Focus Point

////////////

Although it is difficult to acknowledge our sins and failings, over the years life offers many chances to do so. We cannot underestimate the value of an honest estimate of our actual state and its promise of a better day ahead. In order to recognize the truth about herself, Dorothy embraced voluntary poverty. But admitting her life's shortcomings was only part of her story. There are "shouts of victory" in "the tents of the just." When we acknowledge and accept our vulnerability and sinfulness, our human weakness is replaced with divine power. As Paul taught, God's strength is truly made perfect in human weakness. By attending always to her own human frailty and her utter dependence upon the just and merciful God, Dorothy lived that truth.

/////////////

Poverty is a strange and elusive thing. I have tried to write about it, its joys and its sorrows, for thirty years now; and I could probably write about it for another thirty without conveying what I feel about it as well as I would like. I condemn poverty and I advocate it; poverty is simple and complex at once; it is a social phenomenon and a personal matter. Poverty is an elusive thing, and a paradoxical one.

Loaves and Fishes, 163

/////////////////

*D*ay's life offers hope, even surety to those distressed about getting nowhere in prayer or in apostolic labors. She teaches the need for radical patience, persistence, tenacity. She can help us acquire these dispositions when we feel downhearted, when acknowledging honestly how little we seem to have accomplished can leave us discouraged. Dorothy can help us get up again when we feel that we have failed. She lived these same realities, and her life teaches us not to despair, to maintain hope in God's providence and mysterious activity

in our lives, even when we feel that we have
fallen short or failed. In her diaries Dorothy
often recorded dissatisfaction with herself. She
criticizes fiercely the "old woman" who fails to
love even though she has decided to "put on
the new woman," put on Christ.

Dorothy's life gives witness to the paradoxical mystery of New Life issuing from failure
and death. Recognizing and accepting our
poverty, be it physical, moral or spiritual, calls
for Divine Love, summons the Divine Lover
to help us. And for individuals as well as for
society as a whole, help comes. In the depths
of the Great Depression, Dorothy countered its
dreadful fright and want through Jesus—perfect love poured out equally for friend or foe.
God has more than enough love to share.
Strangely, such generosity of spirit emanated
from the lives of two individuals who elected to
be poor, who in reality had to give others only
the God they received. Peter, the peasant philosopher and Dorothy, the activist journalist,
together invited the Holy Spirit's presence and
activity into their own poverty, thereby demon-
strating for many how to satisfy their needs in
a similar fashion. Sharing God's Love through
their own simple human care and compassion
was the right means at the right time to serve
the right ends. Just as in the Paschal Mystery,
out of suffering came healing; out of death, new

life! It requires a patient and yielding disposition to follow such a path of faith, self-denial
and love. The struggle is long and hard, yet the
yoke is easy, the burden light. Even believers,
let alone secular radicals, found these truths
hard to understand or embrace.

Dorothy appreciated the political Left's
vision and legitimate passion for social change,
but she had awakened to the liberating power
of the gospels. Even more, she appreciated
the Church's social teaching and its role in
addressing human suffering. She came to
share her mentor's understanding that "religion was the hope, not the dope, of the people." Nevertheless, all through her long life she
never forgot her politically savvy non-religious
friends' revolutionary critique. She often
agreed with them that unfeeling capitalism
produces economic and human wreckage. Her
new philosophical and theological interpretive
lenses, however, expanded her critique beyond
materialist and class-conflict bases for change.
She set them aside in favor of spiritual and
person-oriented approaches without losing the
legitimate revolutionary fervor for change she
once shared with her comrades. As she grew
in faith, Dorothy knew she had to consider the
inner life. Deep in the heart lay the cause of
good and evil. She knew that the struggling
masses had to become persons with names and

faces and that love of enemy had to supplant
hostility toward the rich and the bellicose.
Again and again, she had to take up not political but spiritual weapons.

Many in the Church held views similar to
Dorothy Day's. In New York City she held up a
picket sign with the words of Pope John XXIII:
"Why should the resources of human genius
and the riches of the people turn more often
to preparing arms...than to increasing the wel-
fare of all classes of citizens and particularly of
the poor?" Yet for the most part she was alone.
Well before Paul VI proclaimed it, Dorothy
knew well from her own sense of things that
"If you want peace, work for justice." Even
though "the arc of the universe" does indeed
bend toward it, justice asks much of us, including great patience and faith. It also requires
that we clarify our values, live more consciously, attentively, carefully. It also requires
great humility. When we fall, we need to know
there is a way to a better place, to remedy poor
choices. Dorothy often chose self-criticism and
penance for herself. Although she found going
to confession difficult, she received the sacrament often, learning there that new freedoms
and hopes need to be born again and again.
Through her acts of penance and hope, she
understood how to pursue better ways.

Photographs

Dorothy Day reading to
Tamar, ca. 1932

Group photo of Dorothy Day, her daughter, Peter Maurin, et al.,
in front of Catholic Worker house on Charles St., NYC, ca. 1935

Dorothy Day
at Maryfarm,
Easton, PA,
ca. 1938

Dorothy Day reading at
Maryfarm, Easton, PA.
ca. 1937

Photographs

Dorothy Day
ca. 1938

Dorothy Day
ca. 1940

Dorothy Day, ca. 1940

Dorothy Day serving soup to Franciscans
at Detroit Catholic Worker, ca. 1951

Dorothy Day 1968

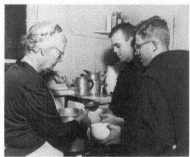

Dorothy Day with Grandchildren

Ultimately, Dorothy fixed her gaze on a treasure that no moth can damage or rust destroy. By choosing not to have far to fall, she found true riches close to the ground of her being. She found security in spiritual treasure, in a house built upon rock, on love. The choice she made brought a grand turn in Dorothy's life, as it can in ours. The Greek term *metanoia* names this turn, the change that leads to finding security in surrender rather than self-assertion. Humility, recognizing one's poverty of spirit, inserts Divine Intention into any tension. Amid her own daunting trials, Dorothy came to recognize that she was beloved. The Perfect Lover casts out both fear and guilt. Her emptiness was filled up with consolation and renewed innocence.

Like St. Francis, Dorothy embraced poverty with enthusiasm. They did not resign themselves to destitution, but sought the spirit of detachment. In Francis, Lady Poverty worked wondrous things. Likewise in Dorothy poverty transformed her desire for wealth from the material to the spiritual. It is in poverty that the treasures of Heaven are more readily received. In poverty, both physical and spiritual, Dorothy discovered herself rich in God's providence and love. Simplicity, she discovered, brought to her life extraordinary balance and harmony.

In accepting chastity, even if reluctantly, Dorothy gave full priority to loving God and ministering to the needy sisters and brothers close to her. She grasped deeply what Jesus meant when he connected all the needy to himself (see Matthew, chapter 25). Dorothy lived a chaste life not because she rejected human intimacy, something she very much desired, but because she chose the Divine Romance and the love of all. Such a choice freed her to live in and build community.

By obeying the gospel mandate to love friend and foe alike, Dorothy set herself free morally. Her principled decision to follow the ancient wisdom of the evangelical counsels allowed her a new liberty to be about loving. Choosing to heed them opened up a more direct, a quicker route to God. Her earlier self-directed, circumstantial, circuitous paths had led to dismay, even despair, but those routes had also led her to God, who now beckoned "Come and follow me." At the same time, Dorothy acknowledged her mixed motives for embracing poverty. We are possessed by our possessions, even our nonmaterial ones. It takes a lot to seek the pure path. Sometimes that pure path begins with recognizing our own impurity, even in our quest for purity. Mary's *Magnificat* echoes that recognition. It is a revolutionary song, a vision and an anthem which declares that it is in our very lowliness that God blesses us and raises us up. Dorothy echoes Mary in her own life's hymn extolling humility and the graciousness of God—the rich are sent away empty and the poor have their fill of good things.

Questions for Reflection

ଔ What connection do you see between voluntary poverty and making Love the priority in your life?

ଔ How do you feel when you recognize your own futility in living the way you know is best, or your failure to live up to your own ideals?

ଔ How can sadness and suffering become more than something tragic in your life, something that generates spiritual growth?

ଔ Voluntary poverty connects us to the Unseen in a most intimate way. How can embracing the poverty and folly of the cross give you a sense of accomplishment?

ଔ When you have suffered or have been called to give yourself away in great generosity (certainly a death to self), what good or promise have you anticipated or experienced?

7

Spiritual Friendship

Focus Point

Dorothy had a natural capacity for relationship. During her early adulthood her secularist and radical friends taught her a lot about the beauty and demands of friendship. Even as her sense of connection with her beloved fellow radicals evolved and changed, those relationships expanded her capacity for friendship. The friendships she made after her conversion brought forth in her a new and explicit spiritual dimension that those she had made earlier could only imply. She moved toward a spiritual vision of the beloved community based on the Christian calling to love God, neighbor and even enemy.

She would help to create and nurture a new community of friends.

/////////////

> We cannot love God unless we love each other. We know him in the breaking of bread, and we know each other in the breaking of bread, and we are not alone anymore. Heaven is a banquet and life is a banquet too—even with a crust—where there is companionship. We have all known the long loneliness, and we have learned that the only solution is love, and that love comes with community.

From the postscript to The Long Loneliness

/////////////

*S*piritual friendship is the *raison d'être* for a book such as this, one that explores how one of God's friends influenced others. Those who are close to God celebrate spiritual giftedness; their distinct witness cannot help but have a profound influence—not only for their peers, but also for those in other places and in other times.

Both as a concept and as a practice, "spiritual friendship" has a long history. The Bible focuses upon the relationship between God and individuals or entire peoples as they are formed in faith, hope and love. Jesus taught that the first commandment is "Love the Lord your God with all your heart, mind, soul, and strength." But the Bible also notes Jesus' second commandment, which is very much like the first. We should love our neighbor as ourselves.

Christian thought and life depends upon the link between these two commands—to love God and neighbor. Dorothy recognized the importance of that tie. Jesus goes even further, telling us to love our enemies, then "ups the ante" all the more when he asks his followers to "love one another as I have loved you." Jesus shows what that kind of love looks like in practice, and how far that love will go to reach the other. These commandments to love like Christ seem impractical, even impossible. But Jesus asks this of us for a reason. He wants us to see things from his perspective. And his perspective is about loving come what may. Dorothy Day understood this well. She struggled tirelessly to live her faith fully.

Dorothy's spiritual friend and guide, Fr. John Hugo of Pittsburgh, led retreats for Catholic Workers, during which he would cite G. K. Chesterton: "The Christian ideal has not been tried and found wanting. It has been found difficult; and left untried."[4] And, "Even watered down, Christianity is still hot enough to boil the modern world to rags."[5] Dorothy Day recognized, as did Chesterton,

Christianity's fundamental and necessary radicalness. Fr. Hugo, and others like him, supported Dorothy's vocation to share the fire, the warmth, the radiance of Christian love. We all need such friends.

People of faith support each other's spiritual growth. The Bible records many blessed exchanges that serve to form Godly individuals. The Bible is filled with stories about persons of great faith and their perspective on the world, as is *The Lives of the Saints,* which Peter Maurin encouraged Catholic Workers to consider their own history book. Just as Dorothy loved the saints and the martyrs and sought to emulate their faith and virtues, we can emulate Dorothy and her life.

Many priests admired her deeply and were moved by her vision and work, her life serving as a guide for their own priesthood. Generations of seminarians and priests were formed through the Catholic Worker movement. In turn, her priest friends influenced Dorothy's prayer life and that of her movement. In *Loaves and Fishes* she wrote, "Our connections with the particular members of the clergy have been very close and, I think, mutually rewarding" (124). Dorothy drew spiritual sustenance from her friendships with Fathers Virgil Michel, John Hugo, Pacifique Roy, Louis Farina, and a host of others. They, in turn, drew inspiration from her.

One notable priest friend of Dorothy and of the Catholic Worker Movement was Virgil Michel, OSB, from Saint John's Abbey in Collegeville, Minnesota. He shared her interest in the link between liturgy and social justice. Like Dorothy, he understood the complementary relationship between the doctrine of the Mystical Body of Christ and a life of prayer and hard work. He encouraged Friendship House, a lay community that was a parallel movement to the Catholic Worker. When he visited the fledgling Friendship House community in Toronto, Fr. Michel consoled and encouraged the downhearted workers. In his biography of Fr. Michel, Fr. Paul Marx presents him in action:

> Destitute, desperate, and lonely, they [Friendship House members] faced a wall of indifference and suspicion, while living and working among the unemployed poor and communists. As yet they had no idea of a vocation as lay apostles. They were ready to quit when Father Michel, sometime in 1934 or 1935, stepped into the bare room of the empty storefront on Portland Street. He sat down on an old broken chair, and seeing their plight, he began as one who understood: "How fortunate you are....This is what I have been dreaming about. You are discouraged. You need the Mass. You must persevere by

all means. You have a vocation. Study
the Mass, live the Mass. Between
Masses, you can bear anything."[6]

Such reassurance that they were on the
right path gave the workers the support and
encouragement they needed to persevere in
their work.

In 1941 Dorothy met Fr. John Hugo during
a retreat he led in Pittsburgh. Echoing Psalm
42, "Deep calls unto Deep," Dorothy was
seeking "a deeper well" and she thought Hugo
could help her draw spiritual waters from the
depths of her prayer life to satisfy her thirst
for interior peace and resolve, for inspiration
and nourishment for her loving yet stressful
social apostolate. Dorothy went to Pittsburgh
because one of the first Catholics she had
befriended, Sr. Peter Claver of the Missionary
Servants of the Blessed Trinity, shared notes
from an earlier retreat with Fr. Hugo. The
knowledge and wisdom in those notes so reso-
nated with Dorothy that she was determined
to find their source so that she could listen to
this priest preach and teach the gospel. After
they had met, Dorothy invited Hugo to give
frequent retreats at the Worker farm. She came
to call them "the bread of the strong," for they
gave workers the strength in spirit and truth
to love God, neighbor, self and enemy. They
were called to imitate Christ and embrace

their own particular crosses in life with courage. Although some criticized these retreats
for being demanding and austere, calling for
heroics and even a severe and questionable
Christian athleticism, they inspired trust in
God and in sacred community. Others, more
partial to organizing and agitating than reflecting and meditating, objected because they
suggested a quietist emphasis, an unsettling
passivity, as it were, in the face of gross injustice. But Dorothy so appreciated the retreats
because she needed them almost desperately as
a source of rest and a wellspring for her grace-
thirsty soul. She urged her co-workers to look
to their own spiritual needs and to slake their
thirst as she did at these springs of grace. The
activity of those in the Worker movement had
to be based on prayer. Action that springs from
such deep sources bears fruit, even if in ways
that the world does not recognize or appreciate.
Fr. Hugo taught the Workers to sow, sow and
sow even more for the good, to imitate Divine
Charity by giving recklessly. This was the
means to a blessed end, to a harvest of justice,
to the ultimate enjoyment of the fruits of love.

Other priest friends included Fr. Conrad
Hauser, a Jesuit missionary who just before
his death arrived at Peter Maurin Farm for a
Lenten season. Fr. Larry Rosebaugh slept in
New York City's homeless shelters at night and

during the day washed pots and pans at the
hospitality house and said Mass. Many priest
friends were strong, able ministers but some
were "down and out" themselves in one way
or another; they too found their place at the
Catholic Worker as special priest guides. The
loving and receptive community buoyed them
up as they struggled with alcohol or sickness,
and they in turn lifted many others up in ways
both mysterious and holy.

Encouragement from sympathetic priests
helped launch the retreat movement that
nourished Catholic Worker members in their
activist commitments. Without a strong spirituality, even visionaries can succumb to defeat.
Virgil Michel and other priests, including John
Hugo and Pacifique Roy, established mutually
beneficial relationships between clergy and
laity. Facing the challenges of the day required
spiritual friendships between attentive and
sensitive priests and generous laypeople. In my
Catholic Worker community in Worcester, Fr.
Bernard E. Gilgun nourished us in Word and
Sacrament, a bulwark that let us stand despite
the contrary winds. Bernie kept up a sporadic
correspondence with Dorothy and let us young
Workers know how much his own priesthood depended on her witness. She treasured
her relationship with these priests, a union of

shared intentions and labors that generated
many spiritual children.

Over the decades, circles of close lay Catholic
friends like Stanley Vishnewski, Marge Hughes
and Rita Corbin, as well as many others, shared
in Dorothy's work. She also maintained friendship with well-known individuals who shared
her vision and met with many of them in person. Mother Teresa visited her at Maryhouse,
and she met many other kindred spirits and
dear friends in their shared struggle: Coretta
Scott King; Cesar Chavez; Catherine de Hueck
Doherty, founder of Friendship House; Sicilian
social reformer Danilo Dolci; Abbé Pierre,
founder of the Emmaus Project; members of
the Grail international women's movement;
Thomas Merton; Eileen Egan, co-founder of
the American PAX Association; philosopher,
poet, and artist Lanza del Vasto, who Gandhi
had named "Shantidas"—Servant of Peace;
Daniel and Philip Berrigan; Koinonia Farm
founders Clarence and Florence Jordan; married mystics Jacques and Raissa Maritain. For
her, these and others like them represented a
contemporary "communion of saints," a holy
band of exemplars and friends with whom she
prayed and worked.

Questions for Reflection

- os Who are your spiritual friends?

- os With which figures in the "communion of saints" do you feel kinship? How does their example touch your daily life?

- os When has a friend given you a critique that you deserved? When has a friend praised you?

- os How can friends help us grow in our relationship with God and with others?

- os To whom do you extend your friendship?

- os How might your friendship with priests help bring about God's Kingdom ?

8

Love Come What May

Focus Point

Dorothy Day demonstrates how to love others, especially when love does not come easy and our efforts seem to bear no fruit. For her, sanctity represented the way to establishing a blessed social order. She forsook ineffective half-measures that diluted the Christian vocation and brought about no real change. She knew that only love is truly effective, that the saints understood that its fruit, even if unseen, is no less real. "Love is the measure," she taught. Her model of true love meant going beyond self and stooping low to serve, like a mother caring for her children or for a spouse who was sick. That is just how she loved, with a love she knew from within, a way of love she had learned by heart. She learned to trust in God and in Christian nonviolence. Even injustice so blatant that it makes the blood boil does not justify fighting evil with evil. Only good can triumph. Choosing the good requires a radical faith in the "folly of the cross" as the way to reconciliation. She believed unconditionally in the power of the resurrection, which meant to "trust in Him Who judges justly."

///////////////

As I waited for the traffic light to change on my way to the Seamen's Defense Committee headquarters, I was idly saying my rosary, which was handy in my pocket. The recitation was more or less automatic, when suddenly like a bright light, like a joyful thought, the words Our Father pierced my heart. To all those who were about me, to all the passersby, to the longshoremen idling about the corner, black and white, to the striking seamen I was going to see, I was a kin, for we were all children of a common Father, all creatures of One Creator, and Catholic or Protestant, Jew or Christian, Communist or non-Communist, were bound together by this tie. We cannot escape the recognition of the fact that we are all brothers. Whether or not a man believes in Jesus Christ, his Incarnation, his life here with us, his

Crucifixion and Resurrection; whether or not a man believes in God, the fact remains that we are all children of one Father. Meditation on this fact makes hatred and strife between brothers the more to be opposed. The work we must do is to strive for peace and concordance rather than hatred and strife.

The Catholic Worker, November 1936

///////////////////

*T*he most difficult thing Christians are asked to do is to love their enemies. It seems only natural to seek justice by avenging hurt with reciprocal hurt. But Jesus proposes another way; Dorothy embraced his teaching that, in the end, Love triumphs over hatred, good triumphs over evil. Believing in Jesus' mercy did not cause her to no longer feel righteous anger or moral indignation. Year after year she continued to rail against the unfairness and at times savagery with which the powerful treated the innocent. Nevertheless, she chose the way of the cross, a path of suffering love. She kept faith. In the end, she believed, love would win. Because of her steadfastness and long-suffering, even hardened skeptics tempered their criticism or relented completely.

Dorothy was one in a constellation of persons deeply committed to spiritual non-violence. She felt spiritual kinship with Leo

Tolstoy, M.K Gandhi, and Martin Luther King, Jr. She admired Dr. King in a special way. No matter what one faced, the right disposition, the solution to every moral problem, was love. It is easy for pacifists to be convinced of the rightness of pacifism. Living out that conviction is difficult; some would say impossible. To be a principled pacifist can mean putting one's shoulder to a huge and heavy wheel. To do so requires toughness—setting one's face like flint against powerful winds of opposition. Full Christian pacifism requires unconditional love in any situation. Many mistrust such love. Like Jesus, whose own disciples could not grasp the intent and importance of loving everyone, Dorothy was rebuffed. Dorothy's stand on peace was rejected by her contemporaries, including many Catholic Workers who felt committed to the works of mercy but not to absolute pacifism. Such unconditional love seemed foolish.

During the Spanish Civil War Dorothy took no sides, maintaining an unwavering pacifist stance. She called for love of enemies, teaching that the sword kills but the cross gives life. The antidote to war is performing the works of mercy. She did not work for peace in the abstract. She worked actively, adhering unswervingly to the truth that Jesus taught. The Second World War, the so-called "good war," meant enduring even more bitter opposition. Many Catholics supported it, and Dorothy needed courage to maintain her stand against all war and to live out the Gospel of Peace. Fascism, she taught, must be confronted not with guns and bombs but with weapons of the spirit. Even military might could not stamp out such deep-seated evil. True peacemaking demands constant prayer, fasting, and almsgiving. The war divided the Movement; when Dorothy insisted on an official endorsement of pacifism, she risked splitting it. Many male Workers were drafted or chose to fight. Houses of hospitality closed. The movement was suffering, and so was she. She turned to ever deeper prayer.

In 1943, Dorothy withdrew from the movement for a time of discernment. Also, Peter had fallen ill. Increasingly, responsibility for the movement was resting on her shoulders alone. This was a difficult time that saw co-workers and friends leave. It may have seemed to spell the failure of the Catholic Worker, but it led Dorothy to draw ever more deeply upon the "wellsprings of the Savior" and to promote a retreat movement within the larger movement. For the remaining loyal workers she obtained spiritually wise guides. This period of suffering became one of setting down ever deeper roots. Such rootedness helped Dorothy and her diminished but loyal bands of workers endure this very rough patch, when the values she had long espoused were relegated to the margins of Catholic thought and national life.

Her deepening prayer life soon generated the means not only to stand firm on the question of peace but to decry loudly with all the moral clarity and authority of a Hebrew prophet the sin of the Hiroshima and Nagasaki bombings, the sheer evil of Jim Crow and the immorality of the Indochina war. Her lonely witness of opposing state violence seemed to end when America's youth, in countercultural movements of their own, began to emulate and promote the theological and political labors she had undertaken and embraced decades before.

Once again the Catholic Worker vision grew popular. Nevertheless, a heavy toll had been taken; the paper's readership had shrunk to a fraction of its former size. But during the war years Dorothy's bedrock faith in Christ and his teaching never wavered and was renewed when a younger generation understood her message much better than did her own. In 1949 Peter died; Dorothy always attributed the founding of the movement to him. But without her, his blessed and lovely vision would have come to little.

After Peter's death, Dorothy joined Ammon Hennacy in an organized outcry against the

atom bomb. By mid-decade she was leading
civil disobedience campaigns against man-
dated air raid drills. Seeking shelter in the sub-
ways, which a nuclear explosion would turn
into mass crematoria, seemed pointless. The
sole defense against the atom bomb was conscientious refusal to use it. Not long ago I met a
man who grew up in Brooklyn. He recalled an
episode when he was a little boy, as his mother
was taking him into the subway during a drill.
On the way, he saw Catholic Workers refusing
to participate. He tugged at his mother's apron
to tell her he wanted to join "those people over
there" holding signs, who would not go gently
into that subway. Even as a child he recognized
Dorothy's moral bearing. On issues of war and
peace, I too, wanted to be by her side rather
than at any cold or hot warrior's. Although
she seemed to stand alone, many were drawn
to her honest witness against atomic madness.
Dorothy and others were arrested and jailed
repeatedly for non-cooperation with the drills;
eventually, the authorities called them off.

Despite the ire of critics, Dorothy stood firm
on the need for economic justice and peace.
In *The Catholic Worker* newspaper she kept
sounding unpopular but necessary themes.
Her articles had a didactic tone but their harsh
yet necessary truth struck the conscience of
her readers. Christ was to be believed and

Christianity lived in a way that transcended ordinary measures of success or failure. Come what may, she came to love.

Questions for Reflection

- ⌘ What means do you judge to be effective in resolving conflict?

- ⌘ How are the means of conflict resolution linked to the ends they hope to accomplish?

- ⌘ Gandhi said, "An eye for an eye makes the whole world blind." Martin Luther King said, "Hatred cannot cast out hate; only love can do that." What means of conflict resolution do these statements suggest to you?

- ⌘ Dorothy saw that Christ's way of the cross gives life as a means to preserve it, but that the way of the sword takes life in a supposed bid to save or defend it. How can Christians *strive for peace and concordance"* through nonviolence?

- ⌘ How have you seen God defend the nonviolent?

- ⌘ What is the risk of trusting, as Dorothy did, in "God who judges justly" rather than in the strength of arms?

9

Hope over the Long Haul: Investment in a Holy Alternative

Focus Point

Peter urged workers to be not just denouncers but announcers, but Dorothy still felt compelled to denounce injustice and war. She saw it necessary that she decry conditions that needed remedies to prepare readers for Peter's vision, his program of promoting what he called the three "Cs"– "cult, culture, and cultivation"–as the way to a society based on love, graced critical thought and an agriculturally-based village economy. She certainly considered the work of announcing to be important too. The Catholic Worker had denouncing *and* announcing to do, and still does. We can too easily underestimate all the building that has been done and must yet be done in the name of the God of Love. The movement puts less emphasis on bricks and mortar (although the movement does have some good brick houses). The real and lasting work is to shelter each other in the invisible House of Love (God). That house has stood the test of time and still does today. Many have dwelt there. Let us ponder the building that is Love, the Temple that is Christ's Body.

///////////

Before bedtime, around nine, we all gathered together, for the rosary and litany. Outside there was a little breeze in the apple trees sighing around the house. The moon shone down on the hilltop, washing the fields in a soft glow. There was quiet and perfect peace and happiness so deep and strong and thankful, that even our words of prayer seemed inadequate to express our joy. May St. Isidore, patron of farm workers, pray for us and praise God for us!

The Catholic Worker, June, 1936

Let me say here that the sight of a line of men, waiting for food, ragged, dirty, obviously "sleeping out" in empty buildings, is something that I never will get used to. It is a deep hurt and suffering that this is often all we have to give. Our houses will not hold any more men and women, nor do we have workers to care for them. Nor are there enough alternatives or services to take care of them. They are the wounded in the class struggle, men who have built the railroads, worked in the mines, on ships, and steel mills. They are men from prison, men from mental hospitals. And women too. They all are often simply the unemployed.

We will never stop, having "lines" at Catholic Worker houses. As long as men keep coming to the door we will keep on preparing each day the food they need. There were six hundred on Thanksgiving day in Los Angeles. I helped serve there too.

But I repeat – Breadlines are not enough, hospices are not enough. I know we will always have men on the road. But we need communities of work, land for the landless, true farming communes, cooperatives and credit unions. There is much that is wild, prophetic and holy about our work – it is that which attracts the young who come to help us. But the heart hungers for that new social order wherein justice dwelleth.

The Catholic Worker, January, 1972

///////////////

*A*lthough she knew well all that is lamentable in American history and culture, Dorothy remained a sure sister of hope. The "long loneliness," a friend once suggested to me, was a reference to her ongoing struggle (and perhaps our own shared struggle) with selfishness. Her life story demonstrates her radical patience with dying to self and rising to new life, especially the rare and surprising gratitude at its end. Dorothy's life provides a map for those seeking conversion. That is no small gift. Her "long loneliness" is also ours. Many can identify with basic alienation, the personal and social malaise pronounced so sharply in our technologically advanced but morally troubled societies. Every person has known profound loneliness. Many find union with God too elusive or too good to be true. Union with the Divine seems only a dream. Dorothy lifts up a welcome promise, a real possibility. Her hope reveals how she knew intimately a faith that was both tested and rewarded. For Dorothy, as it does for everyone, grace came at a price. Even though holiness is a gift, not an achievement, growing in it costs. It is demanding to cooperate with God's ways, listen for cues in prayer and do God's will over a lifetime, but that is what it takes to be blessed.

As the Catholic Worker movement grew, Dorothy found her own way of life evolving. Its contours included prayer, intellectual inquiry, manual labor, and speaking and writing about her unfolding vision. She strove to meet peoples' actual need in concrete, practical ways. Although she often spoke and wrote about the "primacy of the spiritual," the Catholic Worker was a movement that incarnated—the word means "to embody in flesh"—what the Spirit led them to do: "What we would like to do is change the world—make it a little simpler for people to feed, clothe, and shelter themselves as God intended them to do."[7]

In her prayerful activism, Dorothy Day echoed a woman she loved and admired, Teresa of Avila, who asked and taught her contemporaries to ask: 'Whose hands are God's hands but our hands?" Dorothy challenged the Church to respond to that question. God's hands are our hands—or they should be. She issued this radical call to all persons of good will, but especially to Catholics. We must be each other's keeper. Dorothy taught that we needed to answer the question God asked Cain: "Where is your brother?" The twentieth century, a hundred years of unprecedented bloodletting and fratricide, of willful, callous abandonment of all that brotherhood means and is, answered that question like Cain did: "Am I my brother's keeper?" Dorothy answered differently.

Dorothy embraced and lived out Dostoyevsky's bold claim that "all men are brothers." Doing so, she worked indefatigably to propagate a mighty love. She sought to let God's universal love work in and through her.

Questions for Reflection

ભ When have you struggled with your own selfishness?

ભ How do you feel when you set aside others' needs and put yours first?

ભ Recall an experience in which you overcome your self-centeredness by working generously with grace given to you.

ભ How are the spiritual needs of your brothers and sisters connected with their material well-being?

10

A Self-Critical Stance that Leads to Holiness

Focus Point

/////////////

In Dorothy's world view, moral integrity is paramount. Jewish prophets and Jesus himself invited, even goaded, believers to exercise moral truth and justice. Dorothy accepted these invitations with utmost seriousness, but came to recognize that adhering to these teachings was impossible without grace. She learned especially that we must try as hard as we can, but that success depends not on our own efforts and merits, but ultimately on God's gratuitousness. God gives us the grace to be good, but putting love into practice makes us run up against our own poverty of spirit. Despite our good intentions and sincere efforts, our moral deficits and sin cause us to fall short in reflecting God's rich love and compassion. We should rejoice, then, not so much in our own moral accomplishments, but in God's call to engagement—a most gracious and precious gift. Dorothy's witness highlights this blessed complementarity of exercising our free will despite our limitations, and with divine assistance answering the call to social responsibility.

///////////

We plant seeds that will flower as results in our lives, so best to remove the weeds of anger, avarice, envy, and doubt, that peace and abundance may manifest for all.

As for ourselves, yes, we must be meek, bear injustice, malice, rash judgment. We must turn the other cheek, give up our cloak, go a second mile.

What faith I had I held to stubbornly. The need of patience emphasized in the writings of the saints consoled me on the slow road I was traveling. I would put all my affairs in the hands of God and wait.

From Union Square to Rome, 137

///////////////

*O*ver many decades Dorothy grew as a person of deep and abiding faith. She did not arrive there overnight. We can learn from her about the slow and often painful growth that leads to a life of authentic faith and prayer. Conversion ultimately leads to inner transformation and renewal. Dorothy undertook her journey because of her willingness to exercise self-criticism over and over again. Humility opens the door to sanctity. In her unflinching courage in addressing what she saw as her faults and failings she is a model for all of us to be fearlessly open in our own self-critique. We can improve through self-criticism. Dorothy's honest humility allowed the Spirit to work in her. If we are mindful, the Spirit's promptings will lead us along right paths. Dorothy recognized that she could teach her fellow Catholic Workers about self-criticism, about humility. By depending more and more on grace, she had learned to persevere in working to bring about peace in the world by doing the works of mercy. She wanted to exemplify for her co-workers how, if they prayed for an ever-deeper faith, they too could do what she was doing. She came to accept the fact that, although she hoped they could make long-term commitments without being bound by vows, many in the movement came and went. One of her most faithful adherents, Stanley

Vishnewski, echoed Dorothy's feelings about all the comings and goings in the movement when he quipped, "The gold leaves but the dross remains."[8] Dorothy was disappointed that good workers who she had hoped would stay on kept leaving. Nevertheless, she began, albeit reluctantly, to see the movement not as she had hoped—a permanent way of life for the many who joined or allied themselves with the work—but as a school where individuals, especially young people, could learn important lessons that they could take into their professional lives or vocations. Many were influenced in precisely this way—exploring a life of radical generosity for a season, then moving on. Many made life-long commitments to good work in many fields and settings—education, medicine, art, writing—after attending the Catholic Worker School.

Although Dorothy was indeed a teacher, she sought to downplay her leadership role. She realized that in responding to the call to ever greater faithfulness, many looked to others to lead them. She wanted her "students" to become more and more agile in self-criticism and moral improvement, to take personal responsibility. She knew that personal responsibility could be taught, but that students had to internalize their own inner vision and personal conversion. She tried to remain in the background, but everyone recognized her distinctive moral leadership. Nevertheless, she hoped that those who attended her "school" would learn to follow their own lights in doing right.

Dorothy often pointed out that moral weakness is ingrained in the human condition. The Church teaches that we all struggle with "concupiscence," our inherent tendency to go in the wrong direction. Her own experience reflected the truth that "the righteous ... though they fall seven times ... will rise again" (Prv 24:15-16). She expanded on that passage: "If the just person falls seven times a day, how much more the rest of us?" My co-workers and I noted with some trepidation that if someone of stellar moral witness like Dorothy considered herself unjust, what did that say about the rest of us? For Dorothy, everything was founded on humility.

She saw that anyone's act of love, anyone's willingness to take on some of the world's pain, lifts others up and increases their courage and hope. Buffeted by so many distracting influences, we can easily forget that we must see clearly, live simply, and be "pure of heart." It takes trained ears and for some of us even years of practice to hear truly Jesus' invitation: "Come, follow me." We need to be awakened. It takes trained eyes to focus on the essential. The Church teaches that by exercising the cardinal virtues and praying without ceasing, we reorient ourselves to the new world that Jesus asks us to pray for and help usher in. When we pray the "Our Father" we recognize our bond as children of one Father, brothers and sisters of the one Son who prayed that all may be one in the one Spirit. When we act within this prayer, we limit our distractions, our loneliness, our confinement in prisons of our own self-preoccupation. We discover that we are part of a much larger family than we had realized. Trained vision lets us see a new relationship with God, a new consciousness that replaces our past distraction and confusion. We discover the possibility of a blessed present and future.

Self-critique led Dorothy to refocus herself so as to love God and others better. She resolved to keep growing in love through more and better direct action. By acknowledging her own poverty — a crucial step in embracing radical solidarity with suffering humanity — she began to refine her work of loving, a journey she would continue through the rest of her life. In the same way, she invites us to admit our own shortcomings. By fixing our gaze again on "the things above" we can feel the joy of receiving the divine grace that enables us to exercise such personal virtue in thought and deed that we succeed in inviting the whole world to consider moving with us toward God.

Questions for Reflection

- ☙ How has self-criticism helped you?

- ☙ Why are the saints particularly sensitive to their sins, weaknesses, and failings?

- ☙ What risk do you face by exposing the truth about your "lesser self"?

- ☙ How should you respond to exposing your faults to yourself?

- ☙ How might a healthy self-dissatisfaction lead you to sanctity? How can such sanctity change the world?

- ☙ Seeking sanctity requires self-purification. What can you do to be faithful to that search?

11

The Grace of Persistence

////////////

In "Some," Daniel Berrigan, SJ, describes stages of fidelity to the ways of peace. "Some," he writes "stood up once, sat down." "Some stood up twice," and others "walked two miles" then sat down or walked away, crying out "I've had it." Finally, there are the few who remain faithful and determined over the long haul, who "stood and stood and stood." Many, perhaps most, would stand up for a while. Authentic discipleship, however, calls for steadfastness. Dorothy is one who "stood and stood and stood." She clung to that "amazing grace" celebrated in the hymn, the "grace that brought [her] safe thus far," "the grace [that]will lead [her] home." Of those who so stand, Berrigan writes:

"They were taken for fools,
    they were taken for being taken in.
    Some walked and walked and walked –
    they walked the earth,
    they walked the waters,
    they walked the air."

"Why do you stand?" they were asked, and
"Why do you walk?"
"Because of the children," they said, and
"Because of the heart, and
"Because of the bread,"

"Because the cause is the
    heart's beat, and
    the children born, and
    the risen bread."[9]

When asked, Dorothy gave a similar "reason for the faith" that was in her ("Be always ready to give a reason for the hope that is in you but with respect and gentleness" [1 Pt 3:15]). That faith was the fruit of her ever-increasing dependence upon God. A healthy and creative dependence upon the Almighty frees those seeking to hasten the coming of God's just and merciful reign to work with a more confident spirit. One does not do this work alone or through sheer human effort. It is God's work after all and through greater and greater abandonment to divine providence one can become, more assuredly, an "instrument of God's peace."

//////////////

And, by fighting for better conditions, by crying out unceasingly for the rights of the workers, the poor, of the destitute—the rights of the worthy and the unworthy poor, in other words—we can, to a certain extent, change the world; we can work for the oasis, the little cell of joy and peace in a harried world. We can throw our pebble in the pond and be confident that its ever-widening circle will reach around the world. We repeat, there is nothing we can do but love, and, dear God, please enlarge our hearts to love each other, to love our neighbor, to love our enemy as our friend.

The Catholic Worker, June 1946

///////////////

*D*orothy's life was hard, filled with multiple challenges. Her books, diaries and letters convey how difficult her life really was, but also how sturdy she was, facing each day's hardships with faith. Dorothy's challenges would have intimidated someone fainter of heart. Yet even in the face of such great odds, she reminded herself and her readers to hold on to a joyful spirit. She urges us to take up "the duty of delight," a favorite expression that she borrowed from the Victorian luminary, John Ruskin. We must be undaunted in living beautiful lives even though life can be ugly.

Love does cast out fear, but it costs—often a lot, sometimes everything.

Dorothy often recalled a passage from Chapter 9 of Dostoyevsky's *The Brothers Karamazov,* spoken by the saintly monk Zossima: "Love in action is a harsh and dreadful thing compared with love in dreams." She understood what it meant to love in action. Her realism cuts to the bone, yet she would have us *delight* even in what we have to do, even in what we dread. The downcast can recover purpose and joy by cultivating faith and spiritual sight. She wrote, "The consolation is this—and this is our faith too: By our suffering and our failures, by our acceptance of the Cross, by our struggle to grow in faith, hope, and charity, we unleash forces that help to overcome the evil of the world."[10] She had discovered that by relieving others' pain, she could relieve her own as well as theirs. She lived by another of Dostoyevsky's maxims: "All men are all brothers." In her keenly felt awareness of being connected to others in the Mystical Body of Christ, she experienced genuine human intimacy. By helping our neighbor we help Christ. This most sacred solidarity means to give without expectation of immediate return, to labor with patience and fortitude yet to realize, in the very moment of giving, that love is its own reward, the Body thus blessed and remembered.

Dorothy never ceased inviting God into her own pain and that of others. She understood the receptivity believers needed to savor fully divine assistance. In the mid-seventies she told the editors of Sojourners Magazine, "You have to imbibe faith, hope and love; otherwise you get too discouraged." [11] She knew that the Church's mission included members of the Body doing this imbibing together.

In *The Life You Save May Be Your Own*, Paul Elie compares the vocation to spiritual writing of four influential American Catholic figures: Dorothy Day, Thomas Merton, Flannery O'Connor, and Walker Percy. These loosely bound but spiritually close Catholic literati formed what came to be known as the "School of the Holy Spirit," pursuing sanctity in an age when popular wisdom considered traditional faith and even the concept of the holy irrelevant or insignificant. Elie notes that these authors in some measure had read their way to faith. Their discerning reading led them to such faith that they could present and interpret for their fellow struggling moderns age-old themes: conversion, love, prophetic witness, physical care and holy solicitude for the poor, authentic life in Christ. They offered what they drew from spiritual fonts to help their fellow-seekers embrace faith in a skeptical age. They worked tenaciously to retain the wisdom they had discovered for themselves so as to shed the light of faith upon the darkness and inhumanity of the "atomic age." By sharing faith and friendship they strove to build a spiritual family in which no one felt orphaned or lacking the resources of faith.

Our life of faith requires support from our spiritual forebears as well as from sympathetic contemporaries. When she was young Dorothy began to nourish her soul by reading Russian literary masterpieces, a discipline she continued throughout her life. She conveyed the faith lessons she learned from Dostoyevsky and Tolstoy into the daily round of apostolic labors at the houses of hospitality. The colorful Russian characters, be they ordinary or eccentric, reflected the colorful spirit of the men and women who peopled Worker houses. Soul-centered radical Russian Christianity impressed Dorothy and influenced her movement. The Worker houses became schools of love where students studied with and learned from each other.

In one "Easy Essay," Peter Maurin lamented that schools considered themselves places for studying history, not making it. Dorothy felt the same about her undergraduate education. For her, reading and writing had not just artistic but moral purposes. Texts could illuminate their readers and direct them along a new moral path. The power of the ideas Peter and Dorothy encountered in their wide reading transformed them. Certain characters served as models for moral journeys, and novels with an implicit, didactic quality appealed to her. One such book is Ignacio Silone's *Bread and Wine,* which tells the story of Pietro Spina, a young revolutionary in fascist Italy who for his own safety disguises himself as a priest. As he escapes the police, however, his encounters with danger along his way call forth priestly qualities from him. When he is asked to actually minister to them, he tries to fulfill the requests in order to maintain his disguise. He finds himself becoming an unlikely mediator of grace, but ultimately faces a risk he had not anticipated—a call to Christ-like love. Dorothy must have sympathized with Spina because his spiritual journey so resembled her own, from radical activist to an unusual practitioner of Christian faith. Life in Christ demanded fervor even more intense than did any revolutionary cause. Dorothy acknowledged her vocation and learned how to meet its demands by consulting those who had gone before, and those who were facing the same challenges in the present.

Questions for Reflection

ca Consider that when you deal with your
    sisters and brothers each day you are
    dealing in an equally real way with
    the eternal Christ. What judgment
    do you think you will receive for your
    "lived" love?

ca When does your faith life involve sacri-
    fice and persistence?

ca In what way or ways do you love others
    as Christ did?

ca Where do you find kindred spirits who
    help you remain committed to meditat-
    ing God's love?

12

Living in Christ,
Living in the Church

Focus Point

Dorothy needed the Church and was grateful for it. She considered the Church her mother, who she loved and revered with patience and devotion. Nevertheless, she described herself as an "angry but obedient daughter of the Church." Speaking of the Church's accommodation to and willingness to compromise with worldly power, she once wrote: "As to the Church, where else shall we go, except to the Bride of Christ, one flesh with Christ? Though she is a harlot at times, she is our Mother."[12] She loved the Church, yet felt compelled to rebuke her even with sharp, bitter words. Interestingly, in 2000, at the request of Cardinal John O'Connor of New York, the Holy See declared Dorothy Day "Servant of God," the first step in the process toward beatification and declaration of her sainthood.

//////////////

Here was a great question in my mind. Why was so much done in remedying social evils instead of avoiding them in the first place? ... Where were the saints to try to change the social order, not just to minister to the slaves but to do away with slavery?

The Long Loneliness, 45

I loved the Church for Christ made visible. Not for itself, because it was so often a scandal to me. Romano Guardini said the Church is the Cross on which Christ was crucified...the scandal of businesslike priests, of collective wealth, the lack of a sense of responsibility for the poor, the worker, the Negro, the Mexican, the Filipino, and even the oppression of these, and the consenting to the oppression of them by our industrialist-capitalist order. There was plenty of charity but too little justice. And yet the priests were the dispensers of the Sacraments, bringing Christ to humanity, all enabling us to put on Christ and to

achieve more nearly in the world a
sense of peace and unity…

The Long Loneliness, 133

/////////////////

*D*uring her long walks in Chicago with
her baby brother, before her conversion,
Dorothy noted the incongruity between the
Church's teachings about tending to the poor
and actual practice. Yet she became a member
of the Church and worked tirelessly to bridge
the gap between doctrine and practice. She
knew she needed to do something dramatic
to put into effect what Christians professed
with their lips as works of mercy. Even as a
girl, Dorothy criticized the indifference of the
institutional Church to the suffering she saw
around her. Seeing desperation and economic
disparity up close, she lamented the lack of concrete response by people of faith to the needs of
the disadvantaged. Zealous young people often
overlook evidence of the good, but their analy-
sis and demands also contain a naked, if harsh,
honesty. The beauty of Dorothy's witness lies
in the fact that the same intuitions with which
she criticized in her radical youth made right-
ful demands upon her when she later entered
the Church. As a Christian she sought to
bridge the painful gap between principle and
practice. She came to realize the tensions and

triumphs of a lived faith, the daily reality of passion, death and resurrection. She recognized and pointed out the glaring scandalous faults of the community of saints and sinners that is the Church and their failure to secure social justice, yet she also acknowledged her own sinfulness. She saw in all this a great mystery to be faced and lived.

Dorothy certainly struggled with organized religion. She loved the Church because she loved Christ, but was saddened by its accommodations to the nation state, its compromises regarding mammon, ambition, military adventurism, empire building. She particularly lamented the Church's failure to exercise its prophetic gifts regarding such injustices. As a mutual friend recently remarked to me, Dorothy Day sought a "lively church," and even if she had to do it by herself, she would make that liveliness happen. She could not ask others to do right if she would not do right herself. Assuming personal responsibility for the Church's state of affairs because she belonged to the Mystical Body was a hallmark of her long and brave pilgrimage of faith. Dorothy needed the Church but the Church also needed—and still needs—Dorothy.

Questions for Reflection

- ♋ How would you define your relationship with the Church?

- ♋ How can you be both a devoted son or daughter of the Church, and its critic?

- ♋ How might Dorothy's difficulty with yet loyalty to the Church help you address your own relationship and concerns with the Church?

- ♋ Could a non-believer recognize in you, "See how they love one another"?

13

Saint Dorothy?

Focus Point

////////////

Some love Dorothy Day; others find her prob-
lematic. Nevertheless, her cause for beatification has been advanced, and the Archdiocese of
New York has established a "Guild for Dorothy
Day" (www.dorothydayguild.org) "to spread the
word of her life, work, and sanctity and to docu-
ment her ability to intercede for people in need
of God's healing mercy and assistance." Going
forward, the Church will see whether, through
the prayers of the faithful for her intercession and
her response, Dorothy will be declared another
American-born saint.

////////////

> Don't call me a saint. I don't want to
> be dismissed so easily.
>
> *Dorothy Day*[13]

///////////////

*D*orothy was an exemplary convert, led by the natural to the supernatural. Even in a world she considered unjust, even ugly, the gift of creation gave her new bearings. Hope and love trump disorder and fate. In Dorothy's papers William D. Miller found journal entries that suggest why she embraced Catholicism. Her motive was not some deep impulse to lead an extraordinary life or repent a sinful past; it was her unfettered joy in the gift of life itself. Dorothy accounts for her conversion in the deep joy she experienced in finding the presence of God in the natural world—flowers and shells, birdsong, the smile she saw on the lips of her infant daughter, Tamar.

Dorothy Day is now more widely known among American Catholics, and rightly so. Following her death in November, 1980 at age 84, David J. O'Brien, the distinguished Loyola Professor of History at the College of the Holy Cross and chronicler of American Catholic life, described Dorothy as "the most influential, interesting, and significant figure in the history of American Catholicism."[14] What she learned and what she taught is still appreciated in the contemporary Church. Her legacy is being lived out in the several hundred Catholic Worker houses and farms world-wide that carry out the work she and Peter began. Although Dorothy would find the title "Servant of God" more appropriate than "saint," her cause for canonization has been opened. Interest in Dorothy, her lifetime of good works and her holiness is on the rise. Whether she is declared a saint or not, those familiar with her life story recognize her genuine sanctity. Many admirers and co-workers see her as a saint already, convinced that her witness bears the marks of the truly holy. Others sense that assuring that Day's memory is honored with an official feast day would give proper recognition to her life and to the causes to which she devoted it.

Dorothy recognized the risk in being recognized for her holiness. She did not want to be relegated to a shelf of plaster saints, her life's work reduced to a mere pious image. That is not how she wished to be remembered. Dorothy learned to pray and work in the crucible of her own difficulties, grateful for the joys that surprisingly came her way.

The "school of hard knocks" sometimes left Dorothy grumpy, and the good in her life she saw not as something she merited, but as pure gift. Gratitude for grace is expressed in praise directed to God, not to self. Perhaps she feared that people would mistake grace for virtue. But she was also concerned about her witness being reduced to a private endeavor. She feared, I suspect, being presented as more pious than principled, more domesticated and tamed than a thorn in the side of the greedy and warlike. Distant admirers might soft pedal the fact that she was, indeed, the leader of a bold and uncompromising social movement that was and remains a gentle yet certain moral threat to avarice, rapaciousness, and bellicosity in the service of profit. She wanted everyone—especially the greedy, the grasping, the violent—to recognize her relentless antipathy toward all enemies of the good, the generous and the peaceable.

To the indifferent, Dorothy called uncompromisingly for conversion of heart and mind and work on behalf of the suffering and the poor. One must always love, Dorothy taught, but the gospel message truly heeded would make tyrants tremble in holy fear. Hers was the "love" of a prophet—healing complemented by a pride-wounding upbraiding. Change does not come through polite responses to injustice and war. A "Saint Dorothy" would not be content with being a passive, sweet heavenly intercessor. The Church, in its wisdom, knows full well the challenge Dorothy presents. Dorothy wanted and needed the Church. The

Church, in proposing Dorothy for sainthood, is acknowledging the world's need for Dorothy's living witness to gospel truth.

Dorothy counted on God's unfailing love. Through her very self, she let shine and refract the Divine Light and Love at her core. That light was a beacon of triumph of the right and the good—the ultimate reconciliation in love of humanity with God and with itself. The Church teaches that asking a saint's intercession and emulating her virtues edifies and enriches the entire Body. Emulating the sterling faith, generosity and intelligence of someone like Dorothy can help us on our own path to sanctity. From time to time she stumbled, but by the grace of God always got up and returned to her path to holiness. She encouraged her listeners and readers to stake their lives on faith and compassion with humility and grace. Her statement, "We love God as much as the one we love the least" [15] has inspired an entire theology and praxis of reconciliation and peace for the present age and for ages to come. Some do fear that widespread admiration of Dorothy would domesticate her, but not those who truly emulate her. They could not help but love with her same fierce, immeasurable, untamable, radical love for God and for neighbor.

Questions for Reflection

- ❧ What do you think sanctity consists in?

- ❧ Do you agree with Dorothy's view of holiness?

- ❧ Do you feel called to be holy? If so, how can you answer that call?

- ❧ How would you respond if people called you holy?

- ❧ What is drawing you to lead a holy life?

- ❧ In light of the invitation to be holy, even saintly, what in your life would you continue? What would you change?

14

Judged By Love

Focus Point

////////////////

Over her lifetime, Dorothy moved from a "long loneliness" to a blessed community. Once she grasped and held the vision of Christian charity, she realized, as did John of the Cross, that "in the evening of our lives, we will be judged by love." [16] We can forget that the reason for living is our loving. We are defined by our choices. In his account of the Last Judgment, Jesus lets us see the consequences of our choices so as to spur us to acts of love and service. We want to be sheep, not goats. If we keep before us the "last things," we can act appropriately. Dorothy had a keen sense that the one who was beyond time would eventually judge time.

One of the greatest evils of the day among those outside the proximity of the suffering poor is their sense of futility. Young people say, "What good can one person do? What is the sense of our small effort?" They cannot see that we must lay one brick at a time, take one step at a time; we can be responsible only for the one action of the present moment but we can beg for an increase of love in our hearts that will vitalize and transform all our individual actions, and know that God will take them and multiply them, as Jesus multiplied the loaves and fishes.

The greatest challenge of the day is: how to bring about a revolution of the heart, a revolution which has to start with each one of us? When we begin to take the lowest place, to wash the feet of others, to love our brothers [and sisters] with that burning love, that passion, which led to the Cross, then we can truly say, "Now I have begun."

Loaves and Fishes, 210

How necessary it is to cultivate a spirit of joy. It is a psychological truth that the physical acts of reverence and devotion make one feel devout. The courteous gesture increases one's respect for others. To act lovingly is to begin to feel loving, and certainly to act joyfully brings joy to others which in

turn makes one feel joyful. I believe we
are called to the duty of delight.

Diary Entry

///////////////

*O*n one occasion, toward the very end of
her life, Dorothy was speaking with Prof.
Robert Coles of Harvard, a friend and visitor.
She told him that she was trying to remember
the important things, the things that mattered
most, but that the task left her flustered. She
wanted to list the values and life lessons she
wanted to pass on before she died, but found
it impossible. Frustrated but still trying to
focus, she found herself pondering Jesus and
his incarnation, and what a blessing it was to
have set her gaze on Christ for so much of her
life. Such attention to Jesus over a long lifetime
(over a "long loneliness") made Dorothy do
what all effective ministry does: "Bring God to
the people and the people to God."

Several hundred Catholic Worker communities worldwide, urban centers and rural
communes as well as hidden homesteads
and family homes, continue in Peter's and
Dorothy's same spirit of love. Dorothy has been
named "Servant of God." The movement's and
Dorothy's recognition, however, are not her
followers' ultimate concern. Love is. Is the
movement still grounded in love for God and

for neighbor? Peter and Dorothy recognized full well the see-sawing in their houses of hospitality and in the movement itself between holy simplicity and worldly complexity. Dorothy once candidly described her homes as more "houses of hostility than hospitality." Life was often chaotic and prospects dim for what Peter had envisioned as outposts of a new social order. They needed help. A Benedictine friend, Dom Virgil Michel, advised Catholic Workers that they would find genuine social flowering only in the sacraments and prayer. Deep prayer would reveal creative approaches to problems. Liturgical worship and personal prayer were the seedbeds of Christ's nonviolent revolution. In both public and private prayer, good could be sown and nurtured into fields of common life.

Dorothy demonstrated that the gospel mandate for Christian life in the modern world focuses on unadorned love and advocacy for the poor. Peter and Dorothy taught us that the personal and the communal dimensions of living serve each other. Workers should become scholars and scholars workers. They repurposed St. Benedict's dictum "Ora et Labora" for the modern world, unleashing an amazing work of reconciliation that in her old age Dorothy observed "is still going on." [17] Love is the end and love is the means.

Questions for Reflection

ଓ What is the quality of your love?

ଓ How would a merciful, peaceful "revolution of the heart," as Dorothy called it, change the way you live deep within, as well as with those around you?

ଓ How can you attend to the personal and the communal as complementary poles of an integrated life?

15

Still Sowing

Focus Point

/////////////

The Catholic Worker movement has become international. The tiny seed planted in New York City has sprouted and continues to grow, with houses of hospitality in Canada, Mexico, Australia, Uganda and in various European nations. Like the mustard seed in the parable, the Catholic Worker movement has spread to welcome "the birds of the air who find rest in its branches" in many parts of the world.

/////////////

If we are rushed for time, sow time
and we will reap time. Go to church

and spend a quiet hour in prayer. You
will have more time than ever and
your work will get done. Sow time
with the poor. Sit and listen to them,
give them your time lavishly. You will
reap time a hundredfold. Sow kindness
and you will reap kindness. Sow love,
you will reap love. "Where there is no
love, if you put love, you will take out
love" —it is again St. John of the Cross.

The Long Loneliness, 252

We must practice the presence of
God. He said that when two or three
are gathered together, there He is in
the midst of them. He is with us in our
kitchens, at our tables, on our breadlines, with our visitors, on our farms.
When we pray for our material needs,
it brings us close to His humanity. He,
too, needed food and shelter. He, too,
warmed His hands at a fire and lay
down in a boat to sleep.

When we have spiritual reading
at meals, when we have the rosary at
night, when we have study groups,
forums, when we go out to distribute
literature at meetings, or sell it on the
street corners, Christ is there with
us. What we do is very little. But it
is like the little boy with a few loaves
and fishes. Christ took that little and
increased it. He will do the rest. What
we do is so little we may seem to be

constantly failing. But so did He fail. He met with apparent failure on the Cross. But unless the seed fall into the earth and die, there is no harvest.

And why must we see results? Our work is to sow. Another generation will be reaping the harvest.

Don't worry about being effective. Just concentrate on being faithful to the truth.

The work grows with each month, the circulation increases, letters come in from all over the world, articles are written about the movement in many countries.

Statesmen watch the work, scholars study it, workers feel its attraction, those who are in need flock to us and stay to participate. It is a new way of life. But though we grow in numbers and reach far-off corners of the earth, essentially the work depends on each one of us, on our way of life, the little works we do.

"Where are the others?" God will say. Let us not deny Him in those about us. Even here, right now, we can have that new earth, wherein justice dwelleth!

"Aims and Purposes," The Catholic Worker,

February 1940

*A*s she approached death, forty years after the "Aims and Purposes" of the Catholic Worker movement had been written, Dorothy could see the results. She took no credit for many aspects of the Catholic Worker vision coming to fruition, attributing the good that was evident in the work to God's Providence. She had the humility and perhaps also the audacity to say that if God meant for the movement to continue after her death, it would. If not, that was all right too. She displayed what spiritual writers call "holy indifference," an attitude of detachment, resignation and submission in all things to the will of God.

It is natural to seek a good estimate of ourselves, a stay against the darkness of being unnoticed or ignored. Dorothy acknowledged the opinions of others but took little pride of place for herself. She indeed did not let her right hand know what her left hand was doing. Like St. Paul, she believed that "If I speak in the tongues of mortals and of angels, but do not have love, I am a noisy gong or a clanging cymbal" (1 Cor 13:1). Christian charity requires that we place ourselves in the background and give credit where it belongs. Our work is to sow the good seed of the gospel, to do God's work by contributing our own unique gifts. All is grace. In each moment, Dorothy raised a song of praise to the good God, the true author of all that is good. She wanted others to pay attention not to her, but to God.

Dorothy devoted her life to fulfilling the great commandments: love of God and love of neighbor. And she also committed herself with equal fervor to a life of thanksgiving for the gifts of creation and redemption. She sought to imitate Christ in her work for social justice as well as in her work of praise, seeking to love as Christ loved. Dorothy once described hell as the state in which one could not love anymore. She knew the empty loneliness of life without love so she headed toward Love Incarnate, who calls his followers to love as he loves. This love led to the cross, to the ultimate gift in and through death to self, the full donation of self in joy. In the logic of the gospel, the soul rejoices to discover in self-giving not the grave but liberation, like a seed bursting its shell—birth, rebirth, ever greater love and life. Loving and living this way was heartening, yet for all its promise the unselfish life remained a constant challenge.

In her book, *Therese*, Dorothy conveyed a truth she felt still needed to be told. At a stage of life many considered at its peak—full of grace and virtue—she did not write about having arrived at perfection or happy contentment or a retreat from the struggle to a life of prayer, although pray more she did. Instead, she wrote: "Love is a science, a knowledge, and we lack it" (VII). In this statement, Dorothy prophesies to those who will follow her, encouraging them to learn this "science." Her life demonstrates what it means to attend Love's school and learn in it. Love's lessons stay forever with its students, who never stop learning. Eileen Egan, Dorothy's close friend and collaborator, wrote a booklet called "Dorothy Day and the Permanent Revolution." That title captures the nature of her work. To transform the world from an armed camp to a society of societies founded on love, a society of genuine and lasting peace, we need a great generosity of spirit. It is students of the science of love who will learn, put into effect, and keep practicing such generosity. Like Dorothy, these women and men are willing to keep at it.

Questions for Reflection

ೞ When has your spiritual and communal life stagnated? When has it grown?

ೞ How does Jesus' parable of the mustard seed make you feel about your own growth?

ೞ When has your preoccupation with results distracted you from your mission to love? How might holy detachment change the way you look at yourself or the way others see you?

cs What is essential in your life? What do you consider your important achievements? How can you recover a sense of worth based in the transcendent?

cs How does it affect you to realize that your faith life and work life might yield their most valuable results only in the future, perhaps after your death?

Epilogue

*W*hat does Dorothy want you, the reader, and me, the writer, to realize as we reach the end of our fifteen-day journey of study and prayer? I would suggest a number of insights she would want to leave with us. As you and I put this book down and take up again our own unique yet connected pilgrimages of "life with the living God in the joyful communion of the saints," we would do well to review and take within us what Dorothy has taught and continues to teach, and perhaps respond by making resolutions. With more determination or inspiration, we might take up a new practice or renew one we have let go.

Through nature and Scripture God reveals himself—perhaps especially to children, who are still filled with wonder about the world and about the holy book. Our own childhood experiences of wonder and natural inquisitiveness can reorient us toward God. So can sin and disorder. Can we be better people of the Book? How would spending more time with the Bible help our spiritual lives? How we take up and live a Biblical world view? Are our own children open to the Sacred? Does their wonder and joy in relating to God show us how we should think and act?

Our horizons and our hearts can expand. Although we need spiritual help, we need not live in the shadows of chronic fear or guilt. God's Love casts out both. If we really open ourselves personally and deeply to the divine love and mercy poured out so freely in Jesus, we can more aptly encourage a corresponding social reception of the promises of Christ that most assuredly leads to a humanity and creation reconciled to the purposes of God. If we "put on Christ" our lives can be made light, relieved by the sheer joy of his gift. We can open up and widen our lives with the gift of revelation. We can indeed re-present the new creation to others. As people perpetually renewed by Divine Love, we can have words of thanks ever on our lips.

Dorothy tells us that imitating Christ will make us suffer real death when we embrace the "folly of the cross," but it will also make us new.

Imitating God's reckless love, unconditional and unilateral, has a cost. Discipleship will cost. But we will find the strength to embrace the crosses in our lives if we never forget that it all ends in glory. Love as means serves Love as end. Dorothy often quoted Saint Catherine of Siena, "All the way to Heaven is Heaven... because He said: I am the Way."[18] They are tied—cross and crown, death and New Life.

Imitating Dorothy means embracing non-violent love for all despite our own shortcomings and failures. Dorothy knew that virtue untested is easy. Virtue tested is most difficult. Our attempts to direct Divine Love through our human prism may seem insignificant, but they are worthy of the Divine Charity that lies at the heart of life and that gives us chance after chance to repent and believe the "Good News." We are constantly being refined in the furnace of love, but that refining is not merely passive. To be Christ-like, when it is easy and when it is difficult, requires that we cooperate with God's grace. No matter what, we can love better. What spiritual resources do we need to participate more fully in this holy project?

Dorothy reminds us that helping each other to grow holy is holy. To pray, to act, to bring about sacred change—this is the work of the beloved community, which calls its members to ever greater and deeper conversion. We begin with ourselves, but must never stop heeding the call to social as well as personal responsibility.

Dorothy reminds us to take the call to prayer seriously and to live consciously vibrant sacramental lives in the Mystical Body of Christ, the Church. She reminds us that a "society where it is easier to be good" is God's gift, but also something we build together. She reminds us to fix our lives on love, to take it as the pole star by which we orient our lives, keeping in mind that in the end "love is the measure." Can we reset our sights on the prize of love? Can we keep our gaze fixed on "the reign of heaven and its righteousness"?

Dorothy reminds us to seek the will of God and trust him. If we do, we can align our wills with God's and so find our way. Like her, we can bring our restless hearts to him who first brought his loving heart to us. In that great exchange is our precious hope. Do we so hope?

Dorothy reminds us, finally, that in her, as in each member of "that great cloud of witnesses," we have a friend. She does not look down on us from a pedestal, but kneels with us—in simple and devout prayer, as well in a simple and humble gesture of "washing the feet" of our weary sisters and brothers. Dorothy is a constant friend who accompanies us always as we seek a more blessed communion with all the faithful and all of humanity.

Thank you, dear reader, for accompanying me on this pilgrimage. It still goes on. Dorothy would have us live the message of the old civil rights song: "Carry It On." Blessings as, with Dorothy's help, we continue this challenging and wondrous journey!

Prayer for the Canonization of Servant of God Dorothy Day

God our Creator,
Your servant Dorothy Day exemplified the
Catholic Faith by her conversion,
life of prayer and voluntary poverty,
works of mercy, and
witness to the justice and peace
of the Gospel.

May her life inspire your people
To turn to Christ as their Savior,
To see his face in the world's poor, and
To raise their voices for the justice
Of God's kingdom.

We pray that you grant the favors we ask, and
That the virtues of your servant, Dorothy,
May be recognized so that the
Church may one day proclaim her Saint.

We ask this through Christ our Lord.

Amen.

Printed with permission of Dorothy Day Guild,
New York. http://dorothydayguild.org/

Notes

1. Dorothy Day, *The Green Revolution: Easy Essays on Catholic Radicalism* (Fresno, CA: Academy Guild Press, 1961), v.

2. *Selected and New Poems,* (New York, NY: Random House, 1973), v.

3. *From Union Square to Rome*, 9.

4. *What's Wrong with the World*, "The Unfinished Temple," http://www.gutenberg.org/files/1717/1717-h/1717-h.htm#link2H_4_0006.

5. Orthodoxy (New York: John Lane, 1908), 218.

6. *Virgil Michel and the Liturgical Movement* (Collegeville, MN: The Liturgical Press, 1957), 379.

7. "Love Is the Measure," *The Catholic Worker* (June 1946), 2.

8. Dan McKanon, *The Catholic Worker After Dorothy: Practicing the Works of Mercy in a New Generation* (Collegeville, MN: Liturgical Press, 2008), 23.

9. "Some," http://www.nukeresister.org/some-by-daniel-berrigan/.

10. *Loaves and Fishes* (New York: Curtis Books, 1963), 204.

11. Jim Wallis and Wes Michaelson, "Interview-Dorothy Day: Exalting those of Low Degree," *Sojourners* (December 1976), 18.

12. "In Peace Is My Bitterness Most Bitter," *The Catholic Worker* (January 1967), 1.

13. Often attributed to her; see, e.g., http://www.goodreads.com/author/quotes/119043.Dorothy_Day.

14. David J. O'Brien, "The Pilgrimage of Dorothy Day," *Commonweal* (December 19, 1980), 711.

15. *On Pilgrimage* (Grand Rapids, MI: Wm. B. Eerdmans Publishing Company, 1999), 166.

16. *Catechism of the Catholic Church*, n. 1022.

17. *The Long Loneliness,* 286.

18. *On Pilgrimage*, 161.

For Further Reading

Day, Dorothy. *From Union Square to Rome.* Maryknoll, NY: Orbis, 2006. Also available online at The Dorothy Day Library: http://www.catholicworker.org/dorothyday/.

___. *Loaves and Fishes.* (San Francisco: Harper & Row, (1963) 1983.

___. *The Long Loneliness: The Autobiography of Dorothy Day.* San Francisco: Harper & Row, (1952) 1981.

___. *On Pilgrimage.* Grand Rapids, MI: Wm. B. Eerdmans Publishing Company, (1948) 1999.

___ and Francis J. Sicius. *Peter Maurin: Apostle to the World.* Maryknoll, NY: Orbis Books, 2004.

___. *Therese.* Notre Dame, IN: Fides, 1960.

Ellsberg, Robert. *The Duty of Delight: The Diaries of Dorothy Day.* Milwaukee, WI: Marquette University Press, 2008.

Forest, Jim. *All is Grace: A Biography of Dorothy Day.* Maryknoll, NY: Orbis Books, 2011.

McKanon, Dan. *The Catholic Worker after Dorothy: Practicing the Works of Mercy in a New Generation.* Collegeville, MN: Liturgical Press, 2008.

Riegle, Rosalie. *Dorothy Day: Portraits by Those Who Knew Her.* Maryknoll, NY: Orbis Books, 2003.

Also available in the "15 Days of Prayer" series:

Blessed Frederic Ozanam, Christian Verheyde
    978-1-56548-487-0, paper
    978-1-56548-522-8, ebook
Brother Roger of Taize, Sabine Laplane
    978-1-56548-349-1, paper
    978-1-56548-375-0, ebook
Dietrich Bonhoeffer, Matthieu Arnold
    978-1-56548-311-8, paper
    978-1-56548-344-6, ebook
Henri Nouwen, Robert Waldron
    978-1-56548-324-8, paper
    978-1-56548-384-2, ebook
Jean-Claude Colin, François Drouilly
    978-1-56548-435-1, paper
Saint Augustine, Jaime Alvarez García
    978-1-56548-489-4, paper
Saint Benedict, André Gozier
    978-1-56548-304-0, paper
    978-1-56548-340-8, ebook
Saint Bernadette of Lourdes, François Vayne
    978-1-56548-314-9, paper

978-1-56548-343-9, ebook
Saint Catherine of Siena, Chantal van der Plancke
    and André Knockaert
    978-1-56548-310-1, paper
    978-1-56548-342-2, ebook
Saint Clare of Assisi, Marie-France Becker
    978-1-56548-371-2, paper
    978-1-56548-405-4, ebook
Saint Elizabeth Ann Seton, Betty Ann McNeil
    978-0764-808418, paper
Saint Eugene de Mazenod, Bernard Duller
    978-1-56548-320-0, paper
Saint Faustina Kowalska, John J. Cleary
    978-1-56548-350-7, paper
    978-1-56548-499-3, ebook
Saint Francis of Assisi, Thaddée Matura
    978-1-56548-315-6, paper
    978-1-56548-341-5, ebook
Saint John of the Cross, Constant Tonnelier
    978-1-56548-427-6, paper
    978-1-56548-458-0, ebook
Saint Teresa of Avila, Jean Abiven
    978-1-56548-366-8, paper
    978-1-56548-399-6, ebook
Saint Thérèse of Lisieux, Constant Tonnelier
    978-1-56548-391-0, paper
    978-1-56548-436-8, ebook
Saint Vincent de Paul, Jean-Pierre Renouard
    978-1-56548-357-6, paper
    978-1-56548-383-5, ebook
Thomas Merton, André Gozier
    978-1-56548-330-9, paper
    978-1-56548-363-7, ebook

NEW CITY PRESS
of the Focolare
Hyde Park, New York

About New City Press of the Focolare

New City Press is one of more than 20 publishing houses sponsored by the Focolare, a movement founded by Chiara Lubich to help bring about the realization of Jesus' prayer: "That all may be one" (John 17:21). In view of that goal, New City Press publishes books and resources that enrich the lives of people and help all to strive toward the unity of the entire human family. We are a member of the Association of Catholic Publishers.

Also from New City Press

Neighbors 978-1-56548-476-4 $6.95

Chiara Lubich: A Biography 978-1-56548-453-5 $14.95

Road of Hope 978-1-56548-499-3 $16.95

Gospel in Action 978-1-56548-486-3 $11.95

Tending the Mustard Seed 978-1-56548-475-7 $11.95

Going to God Together 978-1-56548-483-2 $11.95

Periodicals
Living City Magazine,
www.livingcitymagazine.com

Scan to join our mailing list for discounts and promotions or go to www.newcitypress.com and click on "join our email list."